you can RENEW this item from
home by visiting our Website at
www.woodbridge.lioninc.org or by
calling (203) 389-3433

GUITAR LESSONS

GUITAR LESSONS

A Life's Journey
Turning Passion into Business

BOB TAYLOR

WILEY

John Wiley & Sons, Inc.

Published by John Wiley & Sons, Inc., Hoboken, New Jersey.
Published simultaneously in Canada.

For general information on our other products and services or for technical support, please contact our Customer Care Department within the United States at (800) 762-2974, outside the United States at (317) 572-3993 or fax (317) 572-4002.

Wiley also publishes its books in a variety of electronic formats. Some content that appears in print may not be available in electronic books. For more information about Wiley products, visit our web site at www.wiley.com.

ISBN 978-0-470-93787-7 (cloth); ISBN 978-1-118-03866-6 (ebk);
ISBN 978-1-118-0386703 (ebk); ISBN 978-1-118-03868-0 (ebk)

Printed in the United States of America

10 9 8 7 6 5 4 3 2 1

I dedicate this book to my partner Kurt Listug,
whose contributions to the success of Taylor Guitars
are equal in every way to mine.

CONTENTS

My cousin, Bob Taylor, asked me to write a foreword for his upcoming book this summer. The request almost coincided with the death of his uncle, Robert Taylor, for whom he most likely was named, so a foreword seemed a just cause. The Taylors are a family who lived the hardscrabble life of Northeast Montana. They are a pragmatic, hard-working, intelligent clan that has married into my mother's family twice. Regardless of our relationship, Bob has written a book that makes one admire his ingenuity and the perseverance of his partners in Taylor Guitars. As a young man, Bob Taylor found his passion in shop class—how to creatively build things—it consumed him. It reminded me of a statement I once saw above a dressing room mirror in an arena in 1970. It simply said: "Make your work your play and play your work"—Sri Chinmoy. Bob's book is an intriguing story of making that concept a reality.

Bob's grandfather, Pierre, whom Bob bears a light resemblance to, was a man of many words. He loved to tell stories; in fact, he wrote a history of his family for the successive generations. Pierre Taylor told stories about living on the homestead land in eastern Montana. He described the survival skills necessary to live on a homestead 100 years ago—the challenges such as traveling by horse-drawn wagons to Canada to catch fish and salting them in barrels to have food stocked away for the winter; making long trips to the woods by the Missouri River to gather enough fuel to survive the brutal winters on the plains. The Taylors spent much of their time scratching out a living, and Uncle Pierre wanted the successive generations to remember the harsh land and life that colored their family's self-determination. What Bob does with his business reflects this determination that made his grandfather proud.

I knew Bob as a youngster only by letters from his mom in our family "Robin." In that day and age, before e-mail, there was a monthly letter sent out called a "Robin" that kept us abreast of the kin. The Taylors were a Navy family stationed in San Diego. Dick Taylor, Bob's dad, was the tallest person in the family until I outgrew him a decade later. On the family ranch there was a pencil mark on the door frame of Dick's height that I later would eclipse. Bob was reported in the Robin to be absorbed in his guitar-making business, which struggles from month to month to make ends meet. What Bob does with his business reflects the same determination that made his grandfather proud.

I called Bob about 15 years ago to ask him about purchasing a couple of guitars as presents for my twin boys. I had heard about how Bob's struggling business had become a successful enterprise and that his guitars were exceptional. My former wife and partner, June, a music fan, while hanging around backstage at a Grateful Dead concert, saw the respect a musician had for his Taylor guitar and sent me on a mission. "Find your boys a Taylor guitar. It would make them a perfect gift." By now, most of my family has a Taylor in their house. Some of them can't play more than a couple of chords (like me) and others have a real feel for playing, but they all love their Taylor made guitars. I thought it might be nice to include a personal testimony from boys-to-adults about their guitars:

> Ben: "Several years ago a friend of mine revealed to me that his father had been a painter and that he himself was a dedicated pianist throughout his childhood. When I asked him why he did not choose a path in the visual arts or in music, he explained that he did not want his art to be heard or seen during the moments of composition. Even the thought of an ear at the wall bothered him; even a distant eye on an unfinished brushstroke

generated discomfort. He told me that he felt most at ease when he experienced a degree of privacy in the composition of his art, which ultimately led him to poetry.

After our discussion, I thought about my relationship with the arts and, in particular, poetry. As a poet, I understood that I, too, value poetry as one of the most private arts. However, during the late hours of the night, when I am not working on poems or when I've grown exhausted by my writing "voice," I often pick up my Taylor 710 dreadnought and find a quiet nook to carve out an intimate bond with my guitar. Those moments provide a crucial outpour, an escape from language."

Charley: "Graduation nears and my father tells me there's a pre-graduation gift waiting in my bedroom; my father houses a four string mini-Martin in Montana, that at 6 foot 8 inches tall, I'll never quite comprehend. I open an oversized box to find my first, my own, guitar: a Taylor CE, cutaway. The spruce wood oiled and rich, contrasted by the rosewood outline, and the mother-of-pearl inlays, is graciously inviting. I tentatively pick up my gift to hear what voice it has, for me and my buddies, around our campfire. A first scale is fingered, a chord strummed, and my love for this instrument is instilled for a lifetime."

Once in a while, Bob comes to LA for business, gives a call, and comes to a game. We wave at each other from the floor to the stands. There is a professional pride in knowing we're both working the same way at a different game. While on a plane, I was reading Bob's account of when he got the "a-ha" moment of knowing that one guitar at a time is the right way to teach his workforce and build the guitars, when one of the Lakers captains, Derek Fisher, got up from his seat and asked me to read a portion of my book from 20 years ago, *Sacred Hoops*, which stated that the repetition of skills that is required of players is what makes the execution of our triangle offense possible. It brings a sense of accomplishment to refine these skills. Reading how Bob found a way to hone the basic techniques of making a guitar down to the easiest possible denominator verified my admiration for his perseverance. There is a way to work and make it enjoyable, and yet dignified, for those who want to have excellence in their work. Bob Taylor has cut that Gordian knot that makes his guitars things to be cherished.

—Phil Jackson

ACKNOWLEDGMENTS

I'm honored to say thank you to a few people for their contribution to this book. To Chalise Zolezzi, who first brought this idea to me and continually bestowed confidence in me during the writing process. To Matt Holt for believing it was a good project and for keeping it interesting along the way. To Shannon Vargo who took stories that I thought were pretty good and made them better.

I'd like to thank Jonathan Forstot, for his good sense, and for naming this book. Thanks to Cory Sheehan and Rita Hoffman for their quality design on the book jacket and photo inserts. And to the staff at Taylor Guitars who are always on my side and help me in every way they can.

A special thank you to my friend and guitar-building mate, Larry Breedlove, for 25 years of guitar building. Nobody could have helped me shape my ideas into real guitars as well as Larry.

And I'd like to thank my wife, Cindy, and my daughters, Minét and Natalie. They are my biggest fans, and have a way of keeping it real. I love them more than Taylor Guitars.

"I heard he plays one of your guitars in it!" said Steve Phillips, my best buddy in those days. "We have to go one night this week, the sooner the better."

Steve and I had been friends for years. It was 1979, I was 24 years old, and we had both been married for about two years by then. We'd met in church, our wives became best friends, and the four of us did everything together.

Steve was more into music than I was, as well as books, movies, and news magazines. He kept me informed. People always thought that since I was a guitar maker I must be an avid musician, and therefore, be in the know of what is going on in the music scene around the world. While there is a bit of truth to that, I was primarily a woodworker with dirty hands and jeans, and a desk piled high with tool catalogs.

However, with my brother-in-law Mike, I played my fair share of music—years' worth, in fact—starting when we were just kids. Mike was Neil Young's biggest fan and together we spent countless hours playing Neil's songs. In fact, I'm sure I've learned more Neil Young songs from Mike than from listening to Neil's records. But I am a fan of Neil's music, and when Steve told me that he heard Neil was playing one of my guitars in his new movie *Rust Never Sleeps*, I had to go.

What 24-year-old, in those days, didn't have memories of driving to high school as a senior in a car with an eight-track tape deck and a copy of Neil Young's *Harvest* playing over and over? We screwed tape decks to the bottoms of our dash boards and put a couple plywood speaker boxes on the floor somewhere, filled up the tanks for 29 cents per gallon and drove to wherever listening to "Old Man," "Heart of Gold," and "The Needle and the Damage Done."

If you're my age, you know what I mean. And when we sold those cars we owned and relieved their back seats of the junk—along with the towels and some swimming trunks, the tools you used to keep the car running, and maybe a hair brush, or a map that was never folded back to its original condition—among the pile of stuff was usually an eight track of Neil Young's *Harvest*.

There was a big theater in the Mission Valley section of San Diego called Pacific's Cinerama. It was one of those huge 70-foot-wide curved screens, and all the big movies played there. When I was a kid, I went with my childhood friend, Greg Robinson, to the movie *Grand Prix* at this same theater. We sat in the front row eating Flix Nonpareils chocolates with the cars racing around us across the big screen. I got so car sick I had to walk to the back. I still can't eat a Flix to this day. Then there was *Star Wars* some 14 years later and now, *Rust Never Sleeps*.

Steve and I scheduled a night and got a few other friends together and we headed to the theater. I was nervous. I hated the anticipation that something was going to happen for fear that it might not. I prefer to drink my disappointment alone, not with an audience of friends interviewing me. Of course, news travels fast when a celebrity buys your guitars. I had been told that Neil Young had bought a Taylor guitar by the dealer who sold it to him. Then, I'd heard from Steve that Neil Young played a Taylor guitar in this movie, but I didn't know it for a fact.

When I walked into the theater, I was met with a flurry of questions:

"Hey Bob, how did you know Neil plays a guitar in the movie?"

"What song does he play?"

"Have you met him; is he a cool guy? Can you get us his autograph?"

"What are you gonna do when you see him play it? Are you gonna just freak out?"

Of course, I didn't have the answers. I was going to find all this out myself, but by the time we'd walked in I was somehow feeling the responsibility to make it turn out good. It was hard for me to bridge that gap between how I felt about it and how everyone else did. They were on my side; I knew that.

We took our seats and I was just hoping that the buddies I was with wouldn't start telling the row in front of us that Neil plays one of my guitars in the movie, because I didn't want to live through it if he didn't.

But he did.

It didn't happen right at the start, it was a while into the film. Every new song he played was somehow a tease to me, waiting to see if this was really going to happen.

Finally, he strapped on the Taylor 855 12-string, put on his harmonica, and walked around the stage, playing "My My Hey Hey (Out of The Blue)" on this glorious guitar and singing. Just him, that 12-string we'd made, and a harmonica.

That guitar was two stories high on that big screen, you could see every detail, it's shape, the name on the peghead, the bridge—it was all there. And the sound would have been George Lucas approved, I'm sure of it.

All at once, I was overcome by a feeling of total satisfaction, alone with myself, soaking in the moment, followed by total embarrassment as my buddies slapped me, looked for reaction, and told people around us that I had made that guitar. Not much has changed to this day in that department.

I walked out of that movie a little more confident, proud that I'd come that far, that I'd made a guitar that Neil Young would buy and play in a movie like that.

The next morning I went to the shop and looked around, realizing that, as great as it was, the night before hadn't changed my life all that much and I still had a lot of work ahead of me if this business of ours was ever going to pan out.

I strapped on my apron and started cutting wood.

GUITAR LESSONS

1 Life's Little Lessons

When I was in the second grade, my grandpa told me that if I were able to shake salt on the tail of a bird I would be able to catch it, easy as pie, if only I could just get the salt on its tail.

This excited me to no end. It was all I could think about, so I got a saltshaker and went outside. Even though I hadn't thought much about it before this, I decided I wanted a pet bird, and wondered who had been keeping this valuable information from me until now. There was something magical about the idea of capturing the mind and body of a bird. I imagined going to school with a bird that sat on my shoulder and ate from my hands. He'd live in my bedroom perched on a stick just waiting to join me in whatever adventure we'd have that day. I couldn't wait to see it up close and to feel the feathers. I wasn't sure how the salt on its tail changed a bird's mind but I was willing to try my grandpa's advice.

I spent the day creeping up on every bird in the neighborhood. I was patient. But soon I learned that most birds weren't really on the ground where I was, and so I started climbing trees, stretching out, waiting, hanging from branches, putting myself at risk. This went on all day and into the next. I was singly focused, and worked toward that reward. Soon I realized that getting the salt on the tail of a bird was impossible for a kid to do. Maybe I was just too young. I wondered if anyone ever really got so close that they were able to actually get that salt on a tail. Eventually, I started tossing salt at birds but that just made them fly away.

After a couple days I asked my grandpa about this and he explained that a bird isn't about to let you get close him, and if he let you get close enough to put the salt on his tail then you were also close enough to catch the bird. I felt a little ripped off, but at the same time I now understood. By then his lesson was making sense and the two days I spent trying to get salt on a bird's tail didn't seem like a waste to me. I had to let the short-lived dream of having a trusty bird-mate fade away, but I thought that somehow I was a little smarter because of it all. In fact I remember telling other kids at the time what I'd been up to and that it really was a bit of a mental trick, a play on words, and I became proud of the fact that I understood the more subtle lesson. They didn't understand because they hadn't spent two days trying to actually do it.

I never regretted the time I spent trying. In fact, I spent a lot of time in thought, and considerable time thinking of other ways one might catch a bird. I even designed and set a couple traps when I figured out how hard it was to get the salt on the tail. I got creative and for those two days, I believed in the goal enough to work pretty hard at achieving it.

It's a funny story to remember at this point in my life, but I do, along with a hundred other stories where I literally dogged it, trying to figure a way to reach my goals. My life is filled with these stories that hold within them precious lessons, advice, and experience. Some are simple, and some took years to unfold, but the experiences went into my quiver, and either a skill, attitude, or habit was put away, to be utilized at some future date. I will share these stories and their lessons in this book.

I often wonder why it is that as children we will work to death on a project, but then as we get older we give up so easily. I realize we are each wired differently, but this pattern is common with so many people. I can't answer the question of why some of us will figure things out and some of us won't, or why some of us will work until we get it and some of us won't, but I can say that those who are willing to work toward their goals and learn, will eventually get there and accomplish something above average.

Nearly all of us can think back to the simpler times of our youth when we were passionate about an idea and worked on it as though we were going to be successful. What if those youthful passions had been nourished and exercised from the very first days? How far along the paths to their dreams would many people be? What if you could help revive or redirect your efforts back into some of the passions and interests that were lost along the way? Or if you could simplify what needed to be done to get closer to where you want to be?

How'd You Know?

Often people ask me how I discovered my passion. It didn't happen that I was walking along and all of a sudden, *wham*, a bolt of lightning came out of the blue. Yet many feel they haven't been so lucky as to hear their calling about what to do with their lives. They express that if they had met their lightning bolt, then maybe they would have more meaningful lives.

Many people think my passion is music, that I'm nuts about guitars and that my life was a long road of playing guitars and becoming an expert on music. Most people who follow that path become famous guitar players, not famous builders. My passion, instead, is making things, understanding how stuff is made, and figuring out how things work.

I've broken nearly everything I've ever owned at one time or another, trying to figure out how it works. There was the folding travel alarm clock that my folks bought me for Christmas that by the next morning wasn't working right because I'd disassembled it. I took it apart and put it back together, and through that I got a great look at the inside of a clock. Maybe the only lesson I learned was to not take a new clock apart, because it never really worked right after that. One might think that was careless and disrespectful, but I disagree. I learned how disappointed I was to have a clock that worked and then a clock that didn't. I also learned to take things apart more carefully in the future. I managed to make it work well enough.

With experience one can learn how to look at things and find out how they come apart and go back together. By learning how other people make stuff, it will help when one day you're learning how to make your own stuff. I've experienced as much as 30-year gaps between learning something and applying it. It's not always immediate.

I also learned that you can't let the speaker wires on your stereo touch each other or they will short out and you might blow the amplifier. There are some amps that will and some that won't. The stereo that I worked all summer to earn the money to buy when I was in seventh grade was one of those that gets ruined when you touch those particular wires together. I found that out just a couple days after buying it while trying to hot-rod some other speakers. I looked at the inside of it for hours, because I'd fixed some similar things like it before by looking and thinking and finally seeing something that was off. But this one needed a pro, so my dad took me to get it fixed. I learned a lot by breaking that stereo—mainly how to be more careful in my exploration. This comes in handy when your car acts up and you have to look and observe carefully to get it going again, and you simply can't afford to break it by careless exploration into the problem. Other people learn different things by breaking something. They learn to stop taking things apart, or they learn to hire a professional, and that professional would eventually be me, or someone like me.

I learned how to take my friend's bicycle brake apart slower and more quietly than I took mine apart, being more observant and more deliberate. Like defusing a bomb in a movie, you have to be quiet and thoughtful and pay attention.

So my story is about how my interest in building things and my interest in playing guitars merged, and how to this day the two burn off each other like two logs in a fireplace. It's about how I took a talent and an interest and combined them into one, where they both could be nurtured and where I could gain satisfaction from the work. And it's about learning to make a living from doing what seems impossible, namely, starting at the beginning, with no assets and working until it grows into something. And there was a lot to figure out, not just the guitar, but the machines, the factory, the employees, the government, the marketing, the sales, the finance, the R&D. I'll say right now that it took two of us, my partner Kurt Listug and myself to tackle all that needed to be learned. Kurt figured out the marketing, sales, and finance, while I figured out the guitars, the factory, and the training of people.

Get in Line

My colleague and friend Greg Deering, of Deering Banjos fame, has been involved with the Boy Scouts of America for most his life. When organizing his troop for an activity he says, "Okay, form two lines. This one on the right is the 'I can figure this out myself line' and the one on the left is the 'I have to have someone show me everything about it line.'"

The amazing thing is that some actually get into the "show me everything about it" line. They do that willingly; they make that decision for themselves, and take the reward that is appropriate for that effort. We all have interests we want to learn about or put effort into and other things in which we're just not interested. When you're involved in something you enjoy, and you're there for a purpose, how much effort do you put forth? For me, there are activities that I am willing to dig into, work toward, and learn about—those are the things I am passionate about.

That willingness to figure out how to do things on my own might have been why I cut the neck off my first guitar. I had no fear of trying things on my own. I also knew that I wouldn't get in trouble for trying. My friends would have gotten in big trouble, but their moms and dads didn't make things like my folks did. My mom sewed clothes and my dad fixed things around the house, built furniture, and worked on the car. My folks also didn't buy me much stuff, so I had to either learn how to make things or earn some money to get it on my own.

There seems to be a lot of formulas for success out there, and most of them are true and have much merit. But one thing that is common to just about all the stories is the positive effect that work and experience has on your success. Now, there are many things that can thwart the work, and they might not be your fault. Nevertheless, people who, one way or another, manage to get a lot of experience in an area of interest usually get good at it.

2 My Very First Guitar

My dad, Dick Taylor, was a seaman in the Navy when I was growing up. He eventually retired as Interior Communication Electrician, Senior Chief Petty Officer, right about when I graduated from high school, but with four kids at home there never was much extra money for my parents to buy all the things we might ask for.

I bought my first guitar from Michael Broward when I was in the fourth grade. He was older than me and already knew how to play guitar. He lived across the street from the house I grew up in and I used to stand in his garage and watch, as he'd strap on that electric guitar and plug into an amplifier on the floor. It was small, maybe knee-high, and he'd plug a microphone into it as well. Then he'd play "Wipe Out" or "Ghost Riders in the Sky" or my personal favorite, "Mrs. Brown You've Got a Lovely Daughter." He even sang the word "douaghtah" just like Herman did.

Next door to Michael was another kid and one day we all ended up in the garage singing folk songs. In fact, they started talking about starting a group, and they even had tryouts. We had to audition by singing "Michael Row the Boat Ashore" to each other. I tried out, but I can't remember if I made the cut. I do remember that we were all still friends the next day.

After tryouts, Michael showed me an acoustic guitar he had and said he'd sell it to me for three dollars. I'm not sure where the money came from but I bought it and took it home. Playing chords was a bit of a stretch for me, and I don't remember learning how to tune the guitar but I do remember learning how to play "Green Onions" on the low strings and "Wipe Out" on the high strings.

At that age, there were forts to build and bikes to ride besides the guitar playing and I made time for all of that as well as building models. I loved watching monster movies on Saturday afternoon TV, and I had all the monster models. There was Frankenstein, Dracula, The Mummy, Phantom of the Opera, and the Creature from the Black Lagoon. I had accumulated a pretty good collection of Testor's Model Paint and some small paint brushes from those models.

This was when I noticed that the white lines along the edge of my little guitar were painted onto the guitar, and that there were some dings and scratches in them. I got out my white paint and a brush and painted over the dings, but the white didn't match. It's amazing how many colors of white there are. Well, the guitar looked worse rather than better so I sanded off the paint I'd put on and the problem grew. Before long I had masked off the entire guitar and sanded all the painted binding away and repainted it totally. This time there were ugly brush strokes so I started over. In all, I think I spent a week and three attempts before I got the white binding painted back on and was satisfied. I should have just left it alone, but that wasn't in my nature.

I spent more time messing around painting and sanding that guitar than I did playing it. But its playing days were numbered once I rode my bike to Apex Music and fell in love with a little electric pickup on a pickguard in the showcase. It was probably twenty-something dollars, but I wanted it bad. I thought that an electric guitar like the one Michael had would suit me better so I would make my acoustic guitar electric. Maybe I had played his and found it easier, or maybe I just thought he was cool, but I think mostly I was interested in the guitar itself. I remember imagining how cool I'd be with a bird on my shoulder at school, but I never remember thinking that about playing guitar. I wasn't interested in guitars to be cool or to impress a girl. I was just interested in the guitar for itself.

There was no sense in buying the pickup right then and I didn't have the money anyway, but that didn't mean I couldn't prepare the guitar. So I took a deep breath and sawed the neck off, trying hard not to ruin the neck in the process. The neck was what I wanted. The acoustic body had to go in order to allow me to put a solid wood electric guitar body onto the neck, add the pickup, and end up with an electric guitar in the end. Some onlooker or naysayer would think it a careless act, but it was filled with care. I planned that neckectomy for days and finally performed it successfully.

Off to the Boy's Club in San Diego I went with my guitar neck strapped to my bike; the one and only bike I ever had in my youth. It lasted me from the second grade all the way to my driver's license. I repainted it four times; I re-spoked the wheels, rebuilt the brakes, and had to find a garage to weld on one of my pedals because the threads of the crank were stripped. I learned a lot working on that bike. In fact, one time I took the Bendix brake apart to service it, but it sprang apart with force when I opened it and scattered its parts on the floor like a pile of marbles. I had to talk Michael Broward into letting me take his apart to see how to put mine back together. He wasn't excited about that. He'd get in trouble if his folks found out, but they never did because his went back together. And armed with the knowledge I gained from reassembling his bike, I fixed mine. I was probably nine years old.

The Boy's Club had a small woodworking hobby shop. Today, they'd probably have a skateboard park or a computer game lab instead, but mine had a band saw and piles of wood. I snagged a big piece of thick plywood and drew an electric guitar shape on it. With some help I sawed it to shape and then the sanding began. I sanded that thing to within an inch of its life. I didn't know how the neck was going to attach or how the pickup would go in, so I just kept sanding it. Eventually, I lost my head of steam because as I tried to figure out solutions to those problems they all looked impossible. Ultimately, I did not finish making that guitar. I really was too young for a project of that scope, and I saved the parts until the next spring-cleaning at the house, and then it was gone.

Whatever it Takes to Get the Job Done

When I was 11, we moved to a new house in a different part of town, where nobody knew me as the boy who sawed the neck off his guitar and ruined it. So with my reputation intact, I arrived at our new place some eight miles away and we started a bit of a new life. I turned 12 years old soon after moving to that house and asked for a new guitar for my birthday. Back then, there was a local store called FedMart that sold neat things at good prices. We found a guitar there.

That guitar probably didn't cost more than twenty dollars. It was a solid body electric guitar, had a chrome pickguard, and a single skinny pickup. A volume and a tone knob made up the rest. All the tuners were on one side of the headstock, and years later, I realized it was a simplified copy of a Fender Stratocaster. I could still only play "Green Onions" and a couple more songs, and I had no amplifier but my dad figured out that we could plug it into the stereo amplifier and I could play through the stereo speakers. Our stereo was homemade from a bunch of stuff my dad collected and put into a cabinet that he built to house it and the TV. It was like one of those consoles you'd buy at a department store but my dad made ours. He built in our old TV, turntables, speakers, and a couple of tube amplifiers, one for each channel of the stereo.

The channel switching knob on the TV acted up and didn't work well. Behind the knob, it looked similar to the bullet holder on a revolver, and there were channel plugs around the cylinder—13 of them—each with a long threaded chamber and a screw that turned inside to tune in a channel. My dad and I uncovered ours when it failed to tune in well. We would manipulate the factory settings and fine-tune the stations ourselves. Our reception was so bad that eventually he made a special tool out of a screwdriver by removing the plastic handle that lived permanently in the TV; touching the metal screwdriver while it was in the tuner, you'd act as an antenna and we'd get good reception. That often ended up being my job. I'd lie on the floor in front of the TV holding the screwdriver and the family would watch. It all made perfect sense to me, and with each funky thing like that in life, I learned a little more about how stuff works. By the time I was 13, I was fixing things around friends' houses.

There were different inputs on the back of my homemade stereo amp, some which amplified the guitar very little and some that amplified it really well. I had to find the right input, and then plug my guitar into it. This was done by lying down on my back, sliding the console out a little and with my fingertips, and plugging in an adapter cord that eventually made its way to my guitar.

That also meant that I had to play guitar in the family room where everyone could see and hear me. I hated that, because I was shy and not a very good player. I didn't advance quickly and had a hard time figuring the instrument out on my own. But over time I learned chords and some songs while playing in my bedroom, unamplified and alone. My friend, Greg Robinson, had an amplifier but no guitar, so sometimes we'd ride tandem on his Stingray bike, him on the front and me on the back holding his little amp, and we'd ride over to my house where we'd plug in and take turns playing.

Music and Shop Class

In the late 1960s, the Beatles had hit the scene and began to change music. Consequently, guitars were becoming more popular. Although I was unaware at the time, when I was about 14, guitars were experiencing one of their highest rises in popularity in decades.

Guitars also became a symbol of rebellion, because most adults did not play guitar. As a kid listening to the radio, you had to learn to play a guitar in order to play and sing the songs you heard. Most parents either didn't understand or thought there was something wrong with the music.

There were a couple of choices when it came to music back then. One was rock and roll, and the other was folk music. I tended to prefer the folk music groups like Peter, Paul, and Mary and the Kingston Trio. But when I was in junior high school, I started listening to Creedence Clearwater Revival and I couldn't get enough of that group. I loved the way John Fogerty wrote songs that were about doing stuff, rather than songs about love. I thought it was unique. I loved that I couldn't understand a word he said and had to work hard to learn the songs. I was the only guy I knew who actually knew the words to "Green River." I later read that Fogerty doesn't care about articulation, but that his lyrics are used as sounds more than words. And I loved that the chord structures were simple and the guitar parts were easy to figure out, unlike Beatles songs, which were more elusive to me.

I grew up in church, in a Christian family, and wasn't rebellious. I liked church, I liked my friends there, and I was happy being a part of the congregation. I liked the music we played in church. But I also wanted to be involved with the music I was hearing on the radio, and so I taught myself to play guitar.

But I didn't know that I wanted to be a guitar *builder* in junior high school. What I did know is that seventh graders could take shop classes and I wanted to sign up. I took drafting, wood shop, and electronics, where I made a crystal radio and learned to draw plans. I made the simplest little jewelry box you can imagine from pieces of redwood and pine, and had several *ah-ha* moments that year about how the most complex looking things were so simple once you learned the method.

In eighth grade, I took metal shop. The shop teacher, Mr. Labastida, loved his job. Shop teachers and teenage boys. This particular camaraderie almost doesn't exist now, but it did back in 1968, and it's one of the essential components of the Taylor Guitars story.

Mr. Labastida was a great metal shop teacher. His lessons and projects were rich and deep and full of potential to learn skill, technique, and design.

By the time I was 14 years old and still in junior high, I knew how to make wood patterns, mix the right amount of water into the right kind of sand, and ram up a sand mold in a flask for casting aluminum. I learned what a sprue and a riser were, and how a match plate and parting compound worked. I learned how to melt aluminum in a crucible and cast it into sand, how to form copper around a male form using hard durometer rubber for the female half of the mold, and how a simple lead strap can take out the wrinkles left behind in the copper. I learned how to forge steel on an anvil, and how to anneal it for easy working, and then how to case harden it using a carburizing compound. I also learned that ground-up leather belts would do the hardening trick if you were fresh out of professional chemicals in the shop. I learned how to heat up a temporizing block of steel and set my case-hardened part on it and watch it turn colors, and then pull the steel block off at the perfect time to obtain the tempering I was after. I learned how to cut threads on a lathe and how to hand fit matching surfaces using Prussian Blue die. I learned how the palm of my hand is about the same as a leather strop and how the final edge of a chisel could be taken to razor sharpness by dragging it backward on my own hand. And amazingly, nobody died in the midst of all this danger.

And yes, I learned how to cook hot dogs on the forging furnace on weekends, when Mr. Labastida would come in to pour some of his personal time into my extracurricular endeavors.

I was good enough in shop class to enter my projects into the California Industrial Arts Exposition in Sacramento. Mr. Labastida required me to make storyboards of my projects when I entered them in the fair. He felt it would help people understand the depth of the project. I attached a full set of plans and actual pieces of the project as it took form, showing the method and progress to a 4×6 piece of painted plywood with a frame. So, in essence, I had to make three or four of my projects to get the parts showing the process to create the finished project.

I was awarded honors, medals, blue and red ribbons, cash rewards, and even plane tickets and hotel stays to attend the fairs and ceremonies. I was the first person I knew to fly commercially in a jet, because I was good at shop. I tasted my first prime rib and horseradish (the latter quite by accident!) on that trip, and I saw projects built by students older than me from around the state that blew my projects away. And I realized there is always another level to strive to achieve. Always.

My work in shop class was recreational. It was fun, and it was what I was living for—to get up and get one of these projects further down the line toward completion. It was play and education at the same time, and I had support, and I didn't have to fight obstacles (usually in the form of adults) to get there. I was lucky, blessed, and fortunate. The timing was right. My parents were supportive. I mean, really; whose parents buy their kids stuff, or watch their kids buy their own stuff and let them dissect it and nearly ruin it? I had motorcycle engines in my bedroom and chemistry sets, which for me meant liquids that, when combined, made fire. Most kids would be in trouble at the first hint of such curiosity. But my interests and curiosities were fed by my parents and the teachers around me allowing me to dedicate myself to the work I loved and thereby hone my skills.

Of course, it goes both ways. My folks trusted me, but I earned that trust.

There is a responsibility that goes along with being a pioneer or maverick. And one of those responsibilities is to not cause needless worry in others. If you're someone who is going to announce your intentions every time you do something, you'll probably not be allowed to do a lot of it. I always felt as a child that there was some leeway in what I told my parents. I didn't need to tell them every detail. But they trusted me and for the most part, that trust wasn't broken.

Tenth grade brought with it my third year in a row of metal shop. Sometime earlier than this, my dad returned from a long deployment to the Philippines. When he arrived he had with him a bunch of furniture he'd made there. While other sailors were visiting town, the bars, or whatever, he had holed up in the woodshop on base and made very nice furniture. I stood on the dock watching the crane unload goods that the sailors had purchased and brought back, and I was proud to see what my dad had made with his own two hands.

There were lot of crates by the end of the day, and piles of mangled 2 × 4s and 4 × 4s, which came off onto the docks. My dad inquired and we were told if we came down we could haul off the wood. We did. We came down the very next day (I'm talking about the next day after coming home from being gone about a year), with a flat trailer rigged behind our 1957 Ford. We pulled nails and loaded crusty 2 × 4s and filled the trailer until it groaned. I think we made a few trips.

A couple of weeks later, we took the lumber to the woodshop at Miramar Naval Air Station, and ran it all through the planer. Then it was back home to build a deck on our house, with a patio roof, and a fancy table and benches, all made from that free scrap lumber. I learned a lot through that experience, and decided that some colonial lamps might look good on the posts of the patio cover. So I made them in tenth-grade metal shop. I also made a wrought iron serving trolley for my mom to put food and goodies on when she entertained back there. It was all ironwork, sheet metal work, and some amber glass on the post lamps. That pretty much took the entire tenth grade, and among other things, I learned how to conceive my own project and see it through to the end on my own. I didn't have Mr. Labastida to help design the project and instruct me, although I would ride my motorcycle back to his school occasionally to ask for his input, because I valued it more than that of my high school teacher.

It's a Family Affair

Once I was in high school, I decided I wanted an acoustic guitar. I was listening to John Denver; Gordon Lightfoot; the Kingston Trio; and Peter, Paul, and Mary, and they all played acoustic guitars. Besides, I still didn't have an amp for my electric guitar. I tried making one once from a broken amp my dad brought home that a sailor had given him. This was just a mono amp head to hook your phonograph up to. I thought it would be cool to build it into a cabinet with a speaker and make my own guitar amp. Well, the amp didn't work, but that didn't stop me. I made the cabinet, learned to cover it with Tolex, put metal corners and bumpers on it just like a real guitar amp, and put a speaker in it. I got some speaker cloth at Radio Shack and when it was done, it looked like a guitar amp. I even wired a $\frac{1}{4}''$-jack into the front like a guitar amp has. The only snafu was that it didn't work. I took that amp apart, tested the tubes, and replaced the bad ones, and still it didn't work. Total failure, but it looked good. So, I really needed an acoustic. My electric days were hurting.

I borrowed twenty dollars from my sister and together with a few bucks I'd saved, I bought a six-string Japanese acoustic guitar. I was in heaven. I was playing a lot better by then, but still didn't have a clue as to how to really play. If you put music in front of me, which they did when I was at church, it meant nothing. I still didn't understand chord progressions or scales. I learned to figure out every chord by trial and error. It was a long time before I could hear chord changes and play easily. My mom could play piano very well by ear, and read music. My little sister could play, too, and she turned out to be a stellar pianist. She has perfect pitch, and can listen to a song and tell you what chords are being played. I can't do that. But one time, my Grandma Taylor sat down when she heard me trying to play a song and just asked, "What chord is that you're playing?"

"It's a G," I said.

"Do you know how to play a C chord?" she asked.

"Yes, like this," I answered.

"How about a D?" she asked.

"Like this," I replied.

And then she guided me through figuring out the song, prompting me to make the simple 1-4-5 changes used in nearly every song. I thought, how the heck does my grandma know how to play the right chords to this John Denver song? I was impressed, totally impressed, and her stock skyrocketed that day.

She was also the one who talked me into playing basketball and going out for the team. It was tenth grade. She said, "Your cousin, Phillip, is doing so well with his basketball, and I think you might be able to be good at it, too. You're not as tall as him, but you're still tall and it's a great sport."

I tried out and I sucked. I can't tell you how relieved I was to be cut. I told Grandma that I got cut, or maybe I didn't because they might have left to go back home to Montana by then, but I was sure relieved to not have to do that. My cousin Phillip, however, did do okay. He played for the New York Knicks. Grandma called him Phillip; you call him Phil. Phil Jackson.

3 Inspiration

In the eleventh grade, I signed up for auto shop. I had my driver's license by then and had bought a Honda 350 motorcycle and was riding it to school. I thought auto shop would be a good next step for me and that I could learn about my motorcycle's engine and work on it myself. One day after school, I rode that bike downtown to another Apex Music location and spied a 12-string on the wall. It was an Eko Ranger, but at the time that meant nothing to me, as I didn't know any guitar brands whatsoever. It had a skinny neck and a thick polyester finish on the top. All in all, not the highest quality guitar, as I learned in later years, but the skinny neck made it easy to play. For a 12-string, that was important. John Denver and Gordon Lightfoot played 12-strings and I decided I should too if I wanted to play their songs. This guitar had a price tag of $175. I didn't have that kind of dough. Not even close. And the idea of asking my folks to buy it for me never entered my mind.

I started thinking, heck, I could make a guitar! I thought it could be fun. I'd only had metal shop classes except for that one semester of wood in seventh grade, and that was a long time ago, but how hard could it be? It seemed simple enough, certainly no harder than the forging, casting, and sheet metal forming I'd done. After all, I'd designed the outdoor post lamps for our deck and succeeded. I went to school the next day and talked to my auto shop teacher. It was September and I was less than two weeks into the class. I told him I wanted to transfer to wood shop and he had no qualms with that.

I went into Mr. Kaiser's shop next door, introduced myself and said that I wanted to take his class and make a guitar. He said, "Great, I have a book for you," and he handed me a copy of Irving Sloane's *Classic Guitar Construction*. Just the thought of that book and the how-to photos within its pages catapults me back to that day even now; it was the first day of all my interests merging onto one path.

There really aren't words to express what I felt like in the days to come after signing up for that wood shop class and looking at that book, thinking about making my guitar. The word that comes closest to describing how I felt is *love*.

The saying, "First comes love, then comes marriage," is not a bad way of describing how a career is formed, developed, and lived out. When you first find something you love to do, there is a honeymoon period, and then there's the work, which includes fights, lessons, heartache, joy, growth, regret, compromise, thoughts of giving up, commitment, and when it turns out good, there's triumph in the end. Of course, there is a good measure of love along the way as well. There is more chopping wood and carrying water in a career, just like in an actual marriage, than there is inspiration and bliss. And if you can't find joy in the work of it, and the trial of it, then it's going to be a long, hard life. So it helps if you are doing something you love.

Every night I went to bed with a guitar part and my book on top of the covers. Each day I got up and could not wait to be able to work on the next steps. It wasn't easy because I was reading a book about classical guitars and building a steel string, 12-string guitar. If you're not a guitar buff, I'll just simply say that these two types of guitars are very different. In my ignorance, I just extracted ideas from the book and applied them in a different way to make my guitar.

The first week of wood shop was learning tools. We had a tool identification test one day. Mr. Kaiser left the classroom and everyone starting whispering, "Hey Taylor, what's number 108?" and I'd look at the mimeographed test and see the tool and say, "Sliding tee bevel" and they'd say, "Cool, thanks." They had no idea what a sliding tee bevel was or what it did. I did though.

Everyone got a pretty good score. But I knew all the names of the tools. I had a knack for tools. I could remember their names. You could drug me and roll me through a factory in a straight jacket on a dolly, like Hannibal Lector, and wake me up later and I'd remember what was there, but I couldn't remember the names of ball players for the life of me.

The next week we were told that we were going to have to learn to draw plans. I thought, ugh, I want to make a guitar, not draw plans or look at pictures of tools. So I went home that night and drew plans for my guitar. I drew top, side, and isometric views. I made a bill of materials. Because of my previous experience making story-boards of my projects when I entered them into the Sacramento Industrial Arts fair, I knew how to present my ideas to a jury.

I went to class the next day, showed my plans to Mr. Kaiser and simply asked if he still thought I needed to spend the next two weeks learning to draw plans. He was duly impressed and I went to work in the shop by myself.

Trust and Respect

I learned along the path of my youth that you can talk to adults and obtain respect. You just need to understand their position, and approach them properly.

Around the same time, some friends and I formed a group that played music in churches. We needed some equipment and we needed a loan to get the gear. I suggested to our group that the pastor of our church might be willing to cosign, as the church, for us to get a bank loan to buy a PA system, a keyboard, and so forth. I called his office and asked if I could meet with him. He said these exact words, "Anything Bobby Taylor wants to say to me, I want to hear."

He cosigned for that loan and we bought $5,000 worth of gear at Apex Music. And we paid back that loan by playing at local churches several times a week for a few years. We usually got paid between $100 and $200 to cover our expenses and so we put that money aside to make loan payments.

The progress on my guitar continued into eleventh-grade wood shop. Mr. Kaiser checked in on me and gave me help, and I went back to Mr. Labastida's shop to make the tools I needed.

It felt amazing to complete that first guitar. I played it and immediately took it over to various friends' houses to show them and their parents. We didn't take a lot of photos in our family in those days, but we took one of me that day. It was the biggest accomplishment of my life to that date, but once it was done I wanted to do it again. One day, a few years later, as I was getting better at my craft, I put a cherry bomb in that guitar and blew it to smithereens. I regret that decision now.

My senior year found me making two more guitars. A matching set, of a left-handed and right-handed guitar—one for me and one for Mike Dwyer, my playing buddy and brother-in-law to be. But the next instrument I would make would not be a guitar.

One day, while driving my parents' 1963 Pontiac Catalina, the song "Dueling Banjos" from the movie *Deliverance* came on the radio. I'd never heard anything like it before. I decided I had to learn to play the banjo. So I did. And I also built one. I could have been a great banjo player; I understand how to play that instrument much better than I do guitar, but I lost interest after a couple years. In those couple years, however, I got pretty good at it and even won a contest. Regardless, I refocused my energy on guitars.

In June of 1973, I graduated from high school. I was 18 years old, and by that time, I'd made three guitars and a banjo. My shop class experience taught me enough to get that far. I knew what I wanted to do, because by the time I was halfway through the first guitar, it became abundantly clear to me that I was going to be a guitar maker. The thing is, I had no idea how that was going to happen. So despite my early cognition of what my life's work was going to be, I stood at that threshold looking across into total emptiness. There was not a single path I could see to get me where I wanted to go. This was not a vocation that anyone in my world had ever even heard of, let alone knew how to get the training for to enter into that field. There was no bright future to look upon, and no example of how to do it. I hadn't even heard of the great guitar companies making guitars during that time. I didn't know what to do next.

I thought I'd go to the American Dream guitar shop, where I bought some of the supplies I needed to build my guitars. I figured maybe I'd go down there and see what I could see.

4 The American Dream

When I began making my first guitar in high school, I didn't know what the different parts were, what they were called, or how they were constructed. That first guitar I bought for three dollars had white stripes around the edges that were painted on. For all I knew, all guitars had painted-on binding. Back then, I didn't even know it was called binding, but in high school I began studying guitars more closely and I decided that the binding must be some kind of plastic that was glued in place. My book, *Classic Guitar Construction*, taught me that the binding on a classical guitar was made from wood strips glued in place, and it also showed me that the frets were made of a material called fret wire. What a revelation that was to me. I felt like I'd cracked some kind of code. Fret wire. Who would have thought?

I had found a local guitar store that advertised guitar repairs and I called them to ask if they had fret wire. They did, and when I was there the owner grilled me as to what I was going to do with it. He actually asked me, "What are you going to do, ruin your guitar?" I sheepishly said that I was making a guitar from scratch and he sort of grunted and sold me a length. While there, I inquired about the binding and found that he had some. So I bought two white plastic lengths and they made their way onto my first guitar.

By the time I began building my second and third guitars in the twelfth grade, I'd discovered another guitar shop located farther away in Lemon Grove, a little town in the east county of San Diego. I rode the 30-minute trip on my motorcycle and was delighted to find a small shop full of benches and a bunch of friendly hippie-types working away on building and repairing guitars. The owner, Sam Radding, was easy to talk to, and he gladly sold me some supplies and invited me to bring in my finished guitars for show and tell. It was there that I discovered I could buy mother-of-pearl in small, gauged pieces ready to saw into inlay shapes. Before that discovery, I was skin diving in La Jolla, catching abalone, eating them for dinner, and grinding the shell down to cut my inlays. On one of those guitars, which I still have today, you can see where it changed from my homemade pearl to the purchased pearl. Mother-of-pearl is made from oyster shell and I was making it from abalone shells by grinding through the colored portions, which is typically saved, into the whiter parts. That part on an abalone is not as white as oyster, and the transition on that guitar marks the spot where I discovered The American Dream guitar shop.

Sam Radding opened The American Dream guitar store in 1970. Sam didn't formally hire employees, but instead ran a very casual co-op. I was 18 years old when I began working there as one of the builders. It was September and I'd just graduated from high school. I couldn't believe that just a few months before I had no idea how I would enter into the business of making guitars and here I was, riding my Honda 350 motorcycle to my job at a real guitar shop.

My guitar-making bench consisted of a frame of 2×4s nailed to the wall and a particleboard top for a work surface. You had to supply your own hand tools, but the shop had a table saw, band saw, planer, belt sander, jointer, drill press, and some routers and orbital sanders. There was also a *spray booth*—an 8' × 16' room with a hole in one end and a fan hung in front of it. I went to Sears and bought my tools: a 6" machinist's ruler, a micro plane, a scribe, a chisel, a little combination square, a narrow back-saw, and a hammer. I was in business.

Sam had a few shapes for guitars, but the two I used the most were the jumbo and dreadnought. They were his adaptations of those popular shapes of the day, and not really direct copies of another manufacturer's guitars. Everyone shared the molds that Sam had made, bending guitar sides over a hot pipe, working them into the shape of the mold an inch at a time. I brought in my own heated pipe bender, which I'd made in Mr. Labastida's shop, and the guys in the shop were impressed. It was a 4″ steel pipe with a clamping strap welded to it so that it could be clamped to a workbench and hung off the side. It was heated with an electric BBQ lighter. It is still used in the factory today for bending wood purfling strips.

Many of the builders who worked there established their own clientele, though sometimes Sam would just send a customer over to a builder. There, guitars had a base price, which was split between Sam and the builder. The builder would then get all or most of the money for adding additional upgrades or options. At the time, a Brazilian rosewood dreadnought's base price was $365. A dreadnought is a style of hollow-body acoustic guitar originally designed by C.F. Martin & Company. The financial arrangement between store owner and guitar builder meant that the builder got $180 to build one, but usually a customer would order another $300 worth of options, like abalone work, wooden binding, or cutaways. In the end, guitar builders could net between $400 and $500 to build a guitar. The percentage that Sam retained helped pay the rent and buy supplies.

Although Brazilian rosewood is highly restricted nowadays, and might carry a premium of up to $10,000 on today's guitar, in those days we bought it locally from an archery bow manufacturer, in lumber form, for $2 a foot. That equates to about $5 for a guitar's worth of Brazilian rosewood.

Developing My Craft

Many guitar players local to San Diego would come, hang out, and order guitars from the builders working at The American Dream. Business appeared to be good from what I could see. I started my first guitar the day I got there, making it on speculation, with high hopes of finding a buyer. I chose to build a maple dreadnought with rosewood binding, maple neck, and rosewood fret board and bridge. It was very exciting to be building a guitar. Without studying in a formal sense, I was learning through Sam's direction how a guitar was designed. For the first time, I learned about how the back was arched and how the set of the neck was positioned in relation to the body of the guitar. I learned about how binding could be designed with wood, and about the significance of the arch in a fret board. Sam showed me various methods and I would tackle each one with enthusiasm. I used my little Craftsman thumb plane and chisel to shape and carve the braces that would be attached to the inside of the body to provide structural strength and enhance the sound of acoustic guitars. The top had a better order to the bracing than any guitar I had made on my own.

The guitar progressed with ease, due to the fact that someone was showing me what to do next, and I was amazed at how easy it was to build a guitar once you knew the process. It looked so professional and legitimate to me at the time.

Sam had developed a unique neck joint, which was a T-shaped mortise and tenon that slid in from the top just like a standard dovetail neck joint. For some reason we all thought that it was easier than a dovetail joint, but in fact, it was pretty hard to make or to remove later if a repair was needed. The only real advantage, and most likely the reason Sam thought of it, was that it could be made entirely with the table saw rather than complicated router fixtures used to make dovetail joints.

Once the neck joint was done, I started on the fretboard. I had to slot it, cut it to taper, round the top surface, fret it, and then dress the frets. Rounding the fretboard was fun. Sam taught me to double-stick tape it, face down, to a long block of wood and set it down on a 6″×48″ belt sander, and then rock it back and forth, working it into a radius. It required a good deal of skill. The mistake most people made was that they just rounded the edges and produced a flat fret board with rolled off edges. Of course, this is not a curve or a radius and would not work well when playing the guitar. To make a radius, you have to *think* radius, and then your brain simply tells your hands and arms what to do. After all that, the fretboard was glued in its completed form to the neck blank, which was then trimmed to the edge of the fretboard with the band saw and spoke shave. Then I shaped the neck on the roller end of the table belt sander, and finished with various files and sandpaper.

My first neck was thinner than standard guitar necks. I just went at it with the file until I liked the feel of it in my hand. People commented on how much they liked it, too. They said it was easy to play and would go on about it like I'd created something brand new. They'd pass it around and say, "Feel that neck! It's awesome; I'm so tired of big fat necks on guitars. How did you figure out how to make a neck so slim?" I'd just shrug, but with each guitar from then on I'd take a little credit and tell them what I was thinking. Then with each guitar, I'd focus on the neck trying to make a good thing even better.

I found a buyer for that guitar and its construction progressed nicely until I dropped it while spraying lacquer late one night, smashing the top portion of it. It was totally ruined, or so it seemed. This knocked the life right out of me and I slid down the wall into a slump for at least 10 minutes, alone in the shop, the doors wide open and the late-night autumn air wafting in. I noticed it was black outside, that I'd been totally unaware of my surroundings, and that maybe I should close the shop doors. I did, and then began to look more closely at the guitar's condition and I found that only the top was broken. I decided that the solution was to remake the guitar right away. I stayed up nearly all night making a new top, removing the old one, gluing it on and then re-binding it. The next day, I sanded it and started the finishing process and ultimately, got myself caught up to where I was the night before. The thing I noticed about that incident was that, when necessary, I was able to get things done at a significantly faster pace.

I spent the next year making about 12 American Dream guitars from start to finish and selling them to customers who happened to stop by the shop. I loved the woodworking portions of the job and sailed right through them. I tolerated the lacquer finishing by putting my head down and just doing it, and I routinely procrastinated on the custom inlay work. It always seemed so tedious to me, but eventually I'd work at it until it was done. That was the part of the guitar where I made money, so I sold this upgrade to customers. I just didn't like doing it. I had to meet the deadlines that we agreed upon and then I had to make sure they were happy when they took their new guitars home. Often, they would return within days for some tweaking and sometimes we'd see what I did poorly, and then I'd have to figure out how to fix those flaws and get the guitars back to them as soon as possible. I worked hard at it and realized that my job wasn't over once I took their money and delivered the guitar. It was over when *they* said it was over.

Working at the shop, I met some musicians and hung around with them, just having fun playing together. One was a girl named Susan who played fiddle and sang like Linda Ronstadt. I thought she was cute, so I played in the same circles where she played. She had no idea who I was. One evening, a group of us were playing for quite a while, and I was having fun and feeling like a part of the group when they broke out the drugs. I didn't have any experience with narcotics, and it threw me totally off balance. I didn't like it, so I faded back into the woodwork. I packed up and slipped out the door. I got in my van and drove home in the pouring rain, feeling kind of lonely, but certainly more comfortable than if I'd stayed there. I tried a couple of other times to be around different groups of people who liked to play music and get high, but it just never worked for me; I always left early and by myself. Meanwhile, I was making guitars and gaining some level of respect for that, and in the daylight hours, when the subject was guitar making, I felt like I was a part of something where my skills were needed and valued.

One of the guys working at American Dream, or The Dream, as it came to be called, was Kurt Listug. He was a San Diego State student, who had a friend named Bob Huff. Bob did electric guitar building and repairs at The Dream and got Kurt a job refinishing guitars. Kurt seemed to enjoy the work enough that he and his friend, Steve Schemmer, who grew up across the street from Kurt, both ended up there doing refinishing work. Kurt and I didn't know each other, but we were in the same place working on guitars.

Another friend of mine named Jerry Peik began working at The Dream, building guitars alongside of me. We drove the 25 miles together each day and enjoyed talking about the guitars we were making. Jerry was a golfer and had thought about becoming a pro, but guitar making also sounded fun to him.

$10,000 and a Dream

Sam had a pair of red socks and believed that when he wore them, money came in. It was a superstition that we all got a kick out of, and there did seem to be a correlation, but there also came a time when the red socks lost their magic. The business hit hard times and Sam was ready to move on. There were some bills that needed paying— namely, a $1,700 bill to Gibson for supplies we had bought. Sam began to talk about closing the shop or selling it to someone who worked there. It was the end of the sixties movement and Sam was very democratic, so he felt that those who wanted to buy the shop should put together a plan and present it to the group, and that the group could vote on who would be the lucky new owner. Sam wanted $3,500 for the business.

The day came when Sam asked everyone who was interested in buying the shop to make their case to Sam as to why they would be the right owners. The builders were divided into two teams: (1) Jerry and me, and (2) Kurt Listug and Steve Schemmer. Jerry was a good craftsman and we had talked about the future and considered buying the business from Sam. My plan for this was pretty simple: We'd buy the business and make guitars and sell them. The rumors around the shop were that Kurt and Steve had actually written a business plan. Evidently, Kurt had gone down to the U.S. Small Business Administration (SBA), met with SCORE (Service Core of Retired Executives), and had gotten a bit of help putting together a plan. In addition, Kurt's dad was a cost accountant for a local aerospace company called Rohr, Inc. and worked with Kurt on developing his plan. They made a pretty good presentation. I can't remember exactly what they said but you could tell they were working on something big. There was something wrong with their plan, however, and it required a little wisdom from Kurt's father to uncover it.

Kurt had approached his father, George, and asked to borrow some money. George had helped with the business plan and was interested in giving Kurt this chance but wanted to know from Kurt if Kurt knew how to build guitars. Kurt said he didn't really know how, so his dad pressed further asking him who was the best builder at the shop. Kurt told his dad about me, and that it appeared to everyone that I was the best guitar maker there other than Sam, so it was suggested as a condition of the loan that Kurt ask if I would join him as a business partner.

A couple days later Kurt asked to have a talk with me. He and Steve sat down with me in the little office of the shop and asked if I would be interested in becoming partners with them. Kurt was interested in running a business and I was interested in building guitars. Kurt and Steve wanted to set up the partnership so that they had more shares than me. They felt that they were inviting me into their business plan only because I could make guitars and that they weren't sure I'd be a good partner. To allow them to have controlling interest, they wanted to have each of them contribute $3,500 and for me to contribute $3,000, setting the shares at 35 percent for each of them and 30 percent for me. I still didn't know Kurt or Steve, but it sounded pretty good to me, so I agreed. I talked to Jerry and he was ready to go try his hand at pro golf anyway, so I joined forces with Kurt and Steve.

Kurt took some of our investment money and hired an attorney to make the transaction legitimate, and to set up a partnership and buy-sell agreement. We officially went into business for ourselves on October 15, 1974. Our initial investment was $10,000; we spent $3,500 to buy out Sam, and $1,500 to pay the attorney to set us up.

That left us with $5,000 to work with. I was 19 and Kurt was 21, as was Steve.

We were in business, complete with drama from day one—mainly because we didn't have the foresight to work out some of the other more minor, but very important details like who owned the phone number to the business before the deal was done. As it turned out, Sam owned it personally, but it was listed in both the White and Yellow Pages of the phone book as The American Dream. Sam's brother also had a retail store with the same name, and he didn't want us to have that number and cause confusion. In fact, he didn't want us to have that name at all. In the end, we lost the phone number and the name, our only leg up for starting as far as we were concerned. We were young and not knowledgeable enough to work out those details before the fact. We had to wait the better part of a year before we could be listed in the phone book. There was no way that a prospective guitar buyer could find us except by word of mouth. Our phone ceased to ring and our shop location was hidden away, completely off the beaten path. We just hoped that the people who already knew we were there would drive to find us again.

We all sat around and tried to think of names for the business. We thought "American Dream" was the best guitar and company name ever, and grieved its loss. We ended up calling our company "Westland Music Company" because we thought we could grow enough to cover the entire *west land*. We still needed a name for our guitars and there was much discussion about calling them "Taylor," but both Kurt and Steve were worried about naming them after me, their new partner who they still didn't know.

I didn't push too hard for the Taylor name, because it was against my nature, but I didn't shy away from it either. It didn't take long for Kurt to come to the same conclusion. Taylor was a good sounding name. It's American, and strong, and the name of a real person, who was actually making the guitars. It could compete with names like Gibson and Martin. Kurt decided for himself that it would be worth the risk in order to launch a company with a potentially strong brand name. I'm not sure what Steve thought, but he went along with it. We kept the name of our business as Westland Music Company and we made Taylor Guitars. Eventually, we dropped the Westland name and just became Taylor Guitars.

As a high school kid, making guitars was simply fun, and required little responsibility from me. It was voluntary and I did it because I enjoyed it. I could have quit at any time and it wouldn't have hurt anyone. Nobody would have thought anything about it. Who would care if a kid started a guitar and didn't finish it?

My American Dream days were just a tiny notch forward with regard to responsibility and I could have walked away pretty easily. Sam would have been okay with that and someone else at the shop would have finished the guitars I'd started. There was usually only one guitar being built at a time by me, sometimes two, so I was only responsible for that customer. It was Sam's problem to pay the bills. It was everyone else's individual problem to do good work for their customers. I had little responsibility, although I had moved from my parent's house by then and had rent to pay.

But in this new partnership, things were different. The business belonged to us now. We'd committed and I was responsible to my two partners, our landlord, the power company, our customers, and my parents from whom I borrowed money to start. It was a whole new level of commitment. Playtime was over.

5 On Our Own

The first day we were in business for ourselves wasn't much different from the day before. We arrived and worked on completing orders that had already been started. Simultaneously, we had to learn guitars, manufacturing, accounting, administration, personnel, leadership, and customer service.

I was 20 years old and had no education beyond high school, but my junior high and high school industrial arts classes gave me six years of intensive training in working with my hands. It was intensive because I loved it and ate it up, spending all my time taking advantage of the opportunity. All the work I did on my guitars related in some way to what I'd learned in shop classes. Because I had already done it, I wasn't afraid of working with steel and aluminum, which also enabled me to create the specific tools I needed to build the guitars.

At the shop, Kurt and I took to each other almost from day one and we seemed to agree on direction and projects for our new little company. Both of us were good at recognizing what was working and what was not, and then making changes. Steve had a more difficult time with this. While I was figuring out how to make guitars and tools, Kurt was figuring out how to sell them. He was also learning accounting with a pencil, ledger sheets, and a calculator. We both had high expectations of ourselves and of each other. We worked together, me teaching him how to build guitar bodies and him sitting down and going over the budget and the reality of our finances with me. Kurt focused on sales, but had to do that while he also helped build the guitars. Steve applied the lacquer finish to the bodies and necks that Kurt and I made and focused more on selling guitar parts. He read books on selling and then would get in his car with a guitar and practice his skills and find us some customers.

Every business is different. While there are some similarities, there are also huge differences: the skill sets required to perform the tasks required, the time and money required before a return is realized, whether a business is location sensitive, and capital equipment requirements, just to name a few. If you're cutting hair, you may get paid four or five times a day, in cash, while only owning a pair of scissors and paying rent on a space. You can make money by washing windows or detailing cars without too much investment or time spent educating yourself. If you're a lawyer, you need to go to school and pass the bar exam. If you're starting out as a guitar maker, you work for a month before you have a product to sell, and then you have to find customers.

While we looked for customers, we did a little repair work here and there to bring in some money, and we sold some tuners, pickups, inlays, and even some wood now and then, but hardly enough to really prosper. The three of us were making cash draws against our capital accounts and hoping that profits would restore those accounts, but the profits didn't come. It wasn't long before our $10,000 investment dwindled to nothing.

When you start a business, you start with a capital investment. The amount of money each person puts in is referred to as their capital account. If you leave money in as you make profit, your capital account, or investment, grows. This is also referred to as equity. If you don't make profit and take money anyway, then your investment, or capital account, shrinks. In a partnership, there might be a partner who can leave more in, or one who needs to take more out because of his personal financial situation. In this way, the investment, or capital account, can become uneven. This could be the first point in which a new partnership can become stressful and cause conflict, as one partner takes out his original investment while the others leave theirs in. In a financial sense, it's unfair to invest and then withdraw your investment. Kurt, being financially minded, kept track of this from the first day.

In November of 1974, just one month after we had bought the business, Greg Deering, who had worked at The Dream but had moved away, returned to town and asked to work for us. He was bringing in a little money by doing all of our repairs. He also built banjos in his spare time. Greg was smart and a little older than me and showed me a couple of new tooling ideas, which I implemented immediately, my favorite being the wood shaper, which can be used to cut shapes from patterns. Rather than drawing a line on every piece of wood I wanted to cut, and then using the band saw and various hand tools to shape the wood to that line, I was able to hand shape a precise pattern, and then the shaper would cut wood against that shape. It was fast, repeatable, and accurate—perfect for producing the same part over and over. Not having the money to buy a shaper, I built two—one that turns left and one that turns right so that the grain of the wood is followed—from mail order parts and surplus motors, and put them to use making necks, braces, and bridges. This was the first time I realized that higher quantity did not necessarily mean lower quality, because the results I achieved were exactly the opposite of that; these were much better parts being produced in a fraction of the time.

Planning for the Future

Throughout our first year, we continued to struggle to find buyers for our guitars. We knew that we would certainly never be able to drum up enough local customers to build and sell guitars for a lifetime. If we wanted to have a future and grow the business from where we were, we needed to develop a line of guitars, sell them wholesale, and forget this local guitar shop idea.

But how do you get a new product onto the market? How do you find out if anyone wants it? How can you be assured that you won't fail? How do you learn what you need to know before you start? The only thing I knew how to do was to jump in, make it, and then sell it. And that's what we did.

We first decided to commit ourselves to one thing and jettison the side businesses like repairs and parts so we were not distracted from our goal. We tried to convince Steve of the wisdom of that move and while he liked the idea of making a line of guitars, he couldn't see the sense in discontinuing our other efforts. We narrowed our focus anyway and this became one of the first situations where the three partners could not agree.

One ingredient that made my partnership with Kurt thrive was that we had similar ideas about business but brought completely different talents and skills to the table. Kurt was better at planning and supervising finances. He also enjoyed selling and marketing. I loved working in the shop and tweaking guitars, and dealing with production in general. I loved learning how to make new guitars. Neither one of us wanted to do the other's job.

While Kurt and I focused on totally different aspects of the business and approached our work in different ways, fundamentally, we saw things in the same light. We knew that abandoning one aspect of the business wasn't the same as abandoning our ultimate goal. We were able to change our minds about what we were doing to get where we wanted to go, whereas Steve felt that every time we said we'd do something, it was essential to hold on to that idea and expend effort toward it, even if it was obviously taking focus away from our main goal. Our main goal, to be fair, was being distilled as we worked, but Kurt and I felt that we were in a sinking hot air balloon and simply had to decide which things in the basket were important enough to stay. We weren't willing to go down in order to save the junk we'd taken when we lifted off. Many of our original business ideas seemed great on our first day when we loaded up to start our adventure, but eventually those things were dragging us down. They had to go. And they were being replaced by something more focused—namely, building a line of guitars.

We began to look into how wholesaling guitars might work. Kurt visited a local store to learn about the cost versus retail price structuring, which was disheartening to hear. We had to either make our guitars more valuable so they could command a higher price or had to take substantially less money for them. We split the difference in our pricing scheme and put a retail value on them that was slightly higher than what we'd been selling them for direct, but then set our wholesale prices lower, figuring we could live with that, even though it was less than we were used to receiving per guitar. Eventually, we believed, we would sell more. The idea was that we would get better and faster and more efficient at making a guitar until that price we were receiving was profitable for us. Kurt and I worked together to pencil out a budget. I'd estimate the time needed to make a batch of guitars while Kurt would figure out the cost of materials and overhead. Had we known how many years we had in front of us before we were successful at these budgets, we might have walked away from it. It's probably better not to know because there is a certain staying power generated by the anticipation of success being just around the corner.

We started talking about the models we would create and what each model would be named. We thought of some not so clever names and eventually decided on a numbering system that would make sense and allow for the addition of new models in the future. We would start with a series that would be in the hundreds, like "800." That would describe the wood and cosmetic treatments. Then, the middle number would designate whether it was a 6- or 12-string, and the last number would be the body shape. The idea worked.

Next, we needed to design the models, so we worked on the 800 series. I made the first 810 with rosewood back and sides, an abalone rosette and ivroid—or faux ivory—trim on the body, fret board, and peghead. I cut a Taylor logo out of mother of pearl, placed it on the peghead, and added some diamond-shaped pearl inlays for the ebony fret board. It was time to sell one. I'd probably made less than twenty guitars at the time and what I was able to do by then was still pretty crude, but not altogether bad. There was a lot of room for improvement on our guitars, but they were certainly good enough to be sold with confidence and pride.

In those days, musical instrument cases were made in the United States. It's a high labor business and has moved to China since, but on its last legs in the mid-1970s was a company in Los Angeles named Geib Cases. Kurt would drive the couple hours up to L.A. and buy a batch of guitar cases. He was showing John Levy, their salesman, some guitars and asking about dealers who might be interested. John liked the neck and thought that our product was unique enough to help our guitars sell. The typical acoustic guitars at the time still had a pretty fat neck and were hard to play. People continually commented that our guitars were easy to play. Kurt learned the names of some guitar stores in Los Angeles from John and made plans to pay them a visit. Our business plan was in motion . . .

Where Plan and Execution Meet

Or so we thought. Acoustic guitars are hard to make and even harder to make profitably. If you can figure that part out, they can then be very hard to sell. Guitar buyers are brand loyal and we were a new start-up company, selling against brands that had been in business for over a century. It took full-time attention and some talent to learn to sell our no-name brand in a marketplace against companies who'd been in full operational swing long before us. I noticed that my friends who owned small guitar companies like ours, but who were sole owners, could concentrate on either sales or production, but seldom both. With Kurt focused on sales and I on building the guitars, we were able to give full-time attention to each side of the business. This was our advantage, and we seemed to make continual progress as time when on. But that progress was slow in the beginning.

Our early ideas of how to run production seemed to make sense and we gave it our best efforts. Our plan was to make 10 guitars in a batch, and finish the batch in about one month. If we could do that and actually sell them, we would do okay, even with the lower prices we were receiving from selling wholesale. The problem was, we barely knew what we were doing. We weren't able to get production working the way it was supposed to. It seemed obvious that we should batch the guitars to take advantage of any setup time. We were new at this, and not just figuring out a workload but also how to correctly *make* the guitar in the first place. We would bend all the sides, then brace all the tops and backs, put the bodies together, and so on, until the batch of guitars was done. But the problem was that we'd have things go wrong that would take a guitar out of the batch; a back would crack, or a neck would twist, or we'd just simply screw one up. We wouldn't want to go back and remake that part because we had already moved on from that operation and were concentrating on something else. The result was that the batch of 10 would have a few casualties along the way and might end up as 7 guitars in the end.

The other thing that made it even worse was that while the batch size was shrinking, the length of time required to make the batch was growing. If we intended to build a batch of 10 guitars in a month, we ended up building six in two months.

Our financial situation was equally bleak. We weren't sure what to do to fix it, but we spent every waking moment analyzing these problems and trying to solve them.

6 Early Successes and Early Failures

We completed our first batch of guitars in the spring of 1975. By that time, we had run out of our initial investment and had no money to spare. Kurt and Steve were both living with their parents and I had gotten broke enough to have to move out of the house I was renting with three other guys. My parents had moved to Spokane, Washington, when I was 19, so I moved in with my sister, Georgi, and her husband, Mike. They lived 30 miles from my shop, so I would scrape money together here and there to buy gas, and I had to take a draw from the company occasionally for that purpose.

This batch of guitars that we had just completed needed to be sold, so Kurt borrowed my van one day and drove to Los Angeles with six guitars in the back. He called on some of the stores that John Levy had suggested and showed them our guitars, face to face.

Kurt called on three or four guitar stores in L.A., including Westwood Music, McCabe's Guitar Shop, and Studio City Music. When he returned late that evening, he pulled out a check from each store. They had all bought guitars from him! This was unbelievable. We did the happy dance for a few minutes and basked in the glory for the next couple days.

Fred Waleki, the owner of Westwood Music, loved our guitars. These were the days of the new L.A. music scene, flowing down from Laurel Canyon. This is where David Geffen made his mark, and the Eagles; Jackson Brown; Linda Ronstadt; and Crosby, Stills, Nash, and Young, were all buying guitars from Fred. More than that, Fred was a benefactor to many of the guys starting out in the late 1960s and early 1970s. Seemingly everyone from those days can tell a story about Fred lending a hand, loaning a guitar, and not worrying about when he'd get paid. Musicians loved him, and some of them ended up buying our guitars from him.

The owner of Studio City Music was also a maker of instruments and Kurt felt that he was just being nice to us, buying those guitars on that day to encourage us and lend a hand. They never turned out to be a long-term Taylor dealer, but even that one sale played a part in our success. Simply by buying those couple guitars, giving us some money and confidence, they helped us to face another day, and we were thankful for it.

McCabe's Music Shop in Santa Monica was right there on the ground floor with us. We couldn't ask for a better dealer of our guitars. When Kurt first walked in, they'd just spent their money on buying some guitars from a larger, more established company. But they seemed to like our attempt, they played the guitars and thought they were cool, and they bought one or two that day, and continued to buy our guitars regularly.

Distribution channels are integral to any business, but a dealer can have a very high level of influence on a budding luthier. Our relationship with Waleki worked well for us. We sent him our best stuff and he sold it. He gave us comments and criticisms about our guitars and we worked on pleasing him with our work. His approval and his business kept us alive for a period of time. If he was not satisfied with our products or would not reorder, it mattered to us, so we listened to his opinions.

Housed in his store was a very good repair shop run by a luthier named John Carruthers. He was larger than life to me at the time. When I'd go into his shop, I'd see road cases from every famous touring band on the music scene. They trusted him with their guitars. My guitars got a little better after I applied some of the things I learned from John.

Our relationship with Fred Waleki provided income, advice, and even ideas on how to actually build our guitars. In the same way that he helped so many fledgling musicians, he helped us as our company started out.

Finishing What We Started

Things went along okay in 1975, except that we were broke, had problems making guitars, there were never enough orders, and dealers would consistently tell us what was wrong with the guitars. In short, it was a rough year. We were living without a paycheck and our families were contributing to our living expenses. I would occasionally take a side job fixing a guitar or cutting wood on our big band saw for a random woodworker or contractor to get gas or food. If any of us made money in any way at the shop, we considered it business income and would deposit it into our business accounts. We didn't have what we felt was our own time. We felt all time belonged to the company, so I would always seek Kurt and Steve's agreement if I wanted to do a side job to earn money to meet my personal needs.

Kurt and I would sit down when he'd reach his stress limit of not being able to pay bills and he'd he say, "If we continue on this path, we'll be out of business in a week or two." I hated those meetings. I would work with a little knot in my stomach much of the time. But work, I did. All day and all night, and we would keep going because someone would buy a guitar and tell us how much they liked it. I also kept going because I had decided that I was a guitar builder, so there was no other career choice for me.

Despite this determination, our resolve was tested every day. Successfully applying the lacquer finish on guitars those first years was one of the most difficult tasks to perfect. We were using finish materials from a reputable, national company and we did our best to make things work, but it seemed that we could never really get guitars done successfully. One time, we finished our batch of guitars and the finish never dried. After curing for the normal week, the finish was still very gummy, so we called in the rep and he suggested heat. We heated them and waited another week, which made no difference and put us another week behind. We waited a couple more days, hoping against hope that something would miraculously happen to dry the finish. We gave up and started the refinishing process, which meant we had to somehow strip the finish off the guitars. We had to use paint stripper on most of them and days later we got all ten stripped and sanded down to bare wood and we were able to start over, with two weeks wasted and a couple weeks' worth of finishing work ahead of us. This was just one of many disasters we faced. It seemed that every time we found one solution, we'd find another problem. These guitars were our sole source of income and it almost destroyed our new business to have the guitars completely built and lose them in the finishing room. The woodworking was easier by comparison. If the finish material was bad or somehow corrupt, we'd never know that until it was too late.

In early 1976, our finish supplier suggested that we discontinue the use of nitro-cellulose lacquer in favor of their more modern catalyzed lacquer. It required a catalyst to be mixed in before spraying, which aided the drying process. The finish was durable and had a good luster and so we began finishing our guitars thinking we might finally have one of our biggest problems behind us. The sample guitars we did looked fantastic. Everything seemed to be working well. Down the street, our friends at Stelling Banjos were using the same finish. We would talk about techniques, share ideas, and compare notes.

Finishing went well for a bit, and then after shipping them out to stores, a guitar or two showed up with cracks in the finish.

The thing about a finish on a guitar is that it requires so much effort to apply, and takes so much time. We would make the body and neck of a guitar in a few days, but then we'd be in the finishing process for two weeks or more. Once the guitar gets assembled, if something goes wrong with the finish, you're sunk. The bridge has to come off, which can ruin the top at times. The neck needs to be removed and that's dangerous as well. Then all this thin wood needs to have the old finish stripped and sanded from its surface and you can't take any of the wood thickness off in the process or the guitar will be wrecked. So, you have a $1,000 product with $5 worth of finish on it, and if that fails, you almost don't recover.

Most finish manufacturers don't put the effort into their products that is needed in order to make it a good finish for guitars. Their main customer makes cabinets or furniture. Compared to other customers, a guitar maker buys very little material. We were a liability to them, but on the other hand, every time they wanted to promote their material they wanted to borrow a guitar for photos.

Weeks passed and more guitars returned with finish cracks. We called Stelling and they confirmed that they were having the same problem. By now, guitars were being returned to us from dealers because of the defective finish. They wanted credit or replacement guitars. This meant that the next few months of work might be shipped for free. We would call in the reps from the finish supplier and they'd advise us to change a method or procedure and continue finishing. In the end, it was a disaster. Stelling Banjos ended up finishing about 120 banjos and we finished several dozen guitars with this particular lacquer. The finish supplier would come in and try to tell us how we were doing it wrong. Of course, we'd used it successfully before, but we were kids, and they were a big company and our testimony was worthless. We were now doing much better application with much worse results. They didn't help us and we felt they were hiding something.

Although we eventually discontinued use of the catalyzed lacquer, we fought this problem for over a year. We knew that every guitar out there was a ticking time bomb. I was surprised that we didn't suffer more of a reputation loss due to this, but customers forgave us and perhaps they were used to it happening with guitars. Many of them never left the factory before we had to refinish them. Others would show up on a dealer's wall with some finish cracking starting to occur. The guitars would trickle in one or two at a time and we'd refinish them. The losses were steep, but it was hard to put a figure to our losses because we were such a new business and weren't profitable to begin with. These types of problems made the uphill climb a lot steeper for us.

We suspected that they had changed the formula, or made some mistake in the mixing of a certain lot that was sold to us. Again, most of their customers for a product like this were cabinetmakers who used two or three coats of finish and would not encounter the same problems as instrument makers who used 12 coats. Fewer coats of finish is more forgiving of bad material, and all finishers know this. None of those customers filed complaints, so the finish supplier argued that it was something in our use or application that was the problem and that none of it was their fault.

Eventually, Geoff Stelling brought a lawsuit against the finish supplier. Geoff was able to prove in court that they had changed the formula to make it unusable for guitars and banjos, and knowing this information, they sold it to us anyway. Stelling had been making money and could prove a loss. They awarded Stelling $100,000 for their trouble. We never sued because we could not prove a loss with no profit history.

It took us nearly 20 years to master guitar finishes and establish a relationship with finish formulators who cared about what we were doing and would work hard to make a top-quality finish for us.

New Opportunities

One day in late 1976, we were so broke that we did not know what tomorrow would bring. Our guitars were getting harder to sell, because even with production problems, we were able to make more than we had developed a market for. All three of us were working late when a customer walked in and asked to look at our guitars. He was interested in one of the guitars we had in stock as well as in having us build him a custom guitar. He also was interested in buying a smaller guitar he could take with him on a trip he was planning to Austria. His name was Charles See and he was the grandson of Martha See of See's Candy. He was the first seemingly rich, well-known person we ever sold a guitar to and he left that night having written us a check for $1,786. That money was enough to buy us another week or two in business. We didn't know what to do about the little guitar, and I asked Kurt and Steve if they minded if I made it myself, as a personal project so I could put the money in my pocket. They agreed and so I made him a miniature rosewood jumbo with fancy bindings and inlays. It had a redwood top, bound in abalone, a miniature mustache bridge and every detail that a big guitar would have. I charged him $500 total for the little guitar, and was happy to get the money.

Our sales slowed down from 1975 to 1976, but we also increased our production numbers. This left us with a few dozen unsold guitars in stock. In the spring of 1976, Paul Rothschild, the record producer for The Doors, approached us. He was part of the very successful L.A. music scene, and he and his brother, Ed, were starting a musical instrument distribution company named Rothchild Musical Instruments (RMI). They had a dream to gather many of the smaller musical instrument manufacturers together and take their products to the retail stores. Rothchild Musical Instruments was born of an interesting business concept. Paul Rothchild had a direct link to many artists because of his position as a record producer. His brother, Ed, had been a salesman in an industrial capacity for many years. They set up a warehouse in San Francisco, and hired an office and warehouse staff and about a dozen independent sales reps to cover the entire country. Rothchild distributed two other brands of acoustic guitars: Larrivée Guitars and Augostino Guitars.

They told us that they had done some research into the market and had noticed our guitars, and also noticed the kind of people who were buying them. They felt our guitars were underpriced in the stores. They told us that they'd buy our guitars at the same price we were currently selling to dealers and mark them up enough for them to make a profit, and then sell them to music stores at that higher price. Theoretically, our sales expenses would be reduced, having only one customer, possibly raising our profit margins and helping our viability. It was a good sounding plan to me, and seemed like a solution. Kurt was more skeptical.

After several days of discussion, we thanked them but said no, and went back to our bleak existence. Kurt, being the cautious one, cast the no vote with the strongest resolve. He felt that we had to create our own future by our own efforts. He also had a sense that just because someone said they could solve our big problem, that didn't mean they actually could. It was just simpler to do things ourselves.

That year was tough, and sales came hard. We built guitars and they went on the storage shelf. Not every one of them did, but the ones that would have been the profit if we could turn them into money. We managed to pay our bills late, very late, but still pay them. We didn't pay ourselves anything, but had a couple employees that we paid on time. We stared at those guitars on the shelf knowing that if we could sell them, many of our problems would cease. It was tough.

Los Angeles became a little too small to take all of our production, so Kurt planned a sales trip to San Francisco. I remembered the night he came back from L.A. with a handful of checks and no guitars. I was expecting the same news as before when he returned with money, but he came back without one single order, and it seemed our business life was over. We continued to work each day building guitars that had no home and seemingly no interested prospects. Kurt would round up a sale here and there, but overall, things were bleak. I would often become stressed and discouraged by all the failure, and by the thought that I would have to give up this dream of making guitars. But then I'd simply get lost in the wonderful ambiance of being in the shop and working on each one of those beauties. Solving the many production problems was my primary focus. The beginning and end of the day were always steeped in disappointment due to the lack of money, but the lion's share of my day was very satisfying. I was easily lost in the pursuit of guitar building.

We always had at least some sales and I would think about that fact. I felt my greatest contribution would be to lower the cost of making guitars by gaining skill and by improving our methods. I thought that even if we never sold more guitars than the level at which we were currently selling, if I could increase our efficiency and lower our costs, we could be profitable. Without a comprehensive plan, I worked on taking care of the obvious time wasters in our production.

During these days, I made some of my more advanced tools like my simple side benders. I'd get my guitar production done for the day and then work late into the night, building tools to help the next batch be more efficient. Improving the guitars and bettering the methods of construction has been the main task of my career. Still, there were many years ahead before I'd make any real progress.

In September through December of 1976, we shipped a total of 34 guitars, which amounted to $18,500 in revenue, or an average of $4,625 per month gross income. This was the end of our second full year of business. We had two employees at the time plus the three of us. That four grand a month wasn't doing much toward paying our expenses, let alone compensating us for our work. But we wanted to build a brand and we believed we would be successful. That belief was challenged over and over, but we pressed on. Quitting was not an option. There just wasn't any talk about that. We owned a business and were serious about it.

Kurt and I began to talk, considering if the Rothchild deal might be in our best interest and by the end of the year, Kurt was on the phone with them, working out a deal. We reached an agreement around the end of the year. It was none too soon, either, because we had no sales. It was our best option at that point. They were willing to commit to monthly minimum orders, which we wanted to believe would happen and we thought, once again, that we could work it out successfully—if we had steady sales we could depend upon. Kurt and I have always been able to make peace with our decisions, and we were happy about this one; we were hopeful for our future. We thought that just maybe, they'd actually come through with sales.

7 Sweat Equity

The Taylor Guitars story progressed through many seasons of highs and lows, as does any successful company. Companies are conceived, born, nurtured, and raised. Some companies live for generations, and some don't, but nearly all have meager beginnings. Ours certainly did, and our beginning seemed to last for years. It's difficult to harvest expert business advice based on our early years, since they piled up with very little progress. We were one step away from going out of business every day. We were utter failures in some ways, in that our business actions did not produce income.

But no matter what picture I paint of the hard years, those days were filled with the satisfaction of mastering my craft. I'm a guitar maker and every day of my life, I was making progress down that road. I had no idea how to make money doing it, and nobody could tell me.

I was blessed with the ability to be happy and content with what I'd been able to achieve, and I mean that in regard to every step of my career. I enjoyed a thousand best days of my life. That's because I can be happy with what I accomplish, even if it's obviously not enough. Knowing that it's not enough doesn't stop me from being happy with the work. But to answer the question of how long it took for guitar making to make me feel good, if anyone wants to know—about a week. A week into building that first guitar I felt so good—I can't explain it. I've already likened it to love earlier in this book. And with each thing I've learned about guitars along the way, whether it's about the guitar itself, how to make them, or how to make progress toward profitability, I've felt great.

I wanted all of our guitars to sound good, play great, and last long without trouble to the owner. I was already making a little name for myself because I designed a nontraditional neck joint. I used bolts instead of a dovetail wood joint to hold the necks onto my guitars. I'd been doing this since the creation of my sixth or seventh guitar. I didn't know any better; I just decided how I wanted to make my guitar, and since I was self-taught, I didn't ask anyone if this was allowable. As it turned out, dovetail joints only became a topic of debate right after I stopped using them. Before I developed the bolt-on neck, there were no alternative methods to compare with what was normally used; the guitar was just a guitar with no real discussion of how the neck was attached. It just *was*. Its virtues were seldom extolled. Repairmen hated dovetails because of the intense work required to remove the neck from a guitar for repair. But the day I built my first bolt-on acoustic guitar neck, all of a sudden dovetail neck joints became something that no guitar could be without, as if it were inspired by Ben Franklin himself and that all other options had already been explored. I invite you to Google "dovetail vs. bolt on" and see how much is written on the subject. I never would have thought I'd be responsible for something like that at 20 years of age.

Talking to a dealer once, we asked, "In your opinion, what does this guitar need in order to be a successful player in the market?"

He pondered for a moment and simply answered, "Time."

There were years where we wrestled with the same things day in and day out. We'd make progress on many fronts, but it wasn't until progress was made on all fronts that the bottom line began to change. All fronts include things like the passing of time.

There wasn't anything we could do about the time factor back then, and we didn't accept that the passage of time was a requirement for our success. We were wrong, of course, but it's a moot point because we had to stay in business in order for the time to pass that would allow people to know who we were, because nobody knew who we were. We weren't brilliant kids, but we were smart enough, and we didn't quit. So we worked. What else could we do? We got smarter as time went on and as we gained experience.

Starting a business was kind of like going to school. Many people spend four years in college, only to go to graduate school for another couple years or more after that. Then they get a job at a company and learn the business before they can be worth much to the employer. From there, they might work at their first job for five years and then start over somewhere else, but all the while becoming a little more capable of making valuable contributions. Ten or twelve years might pass before they feel they're finally getting somewhere. The timeline wasn't much different for us.

Formal education and work experience is a normal approach to becoming a useful addition to the workforce; my path was just an alternate one. People call it the school of hard knocks, or on-the-job training. To be fair, I was working for myself, which I have observed to be one of the greatest sources of motivation.

Start Early and Work Hard

For me, this is the best part of the story because it's something that nearly everyone can do. Everyone can work hard. My friend and bestselling author, John Maxwell, says, "Pay now and play later, or, play now and pay later, but sooner or later you're going to pay." We paid early and I'm glad we did. What we did early in our business was not something of genius, but more a story of having a goal and working to get there. It was fueled by passion and commitment. It wasn't that kind of commitment where we said we were just trying this out to see how it would go, but rather the type of commitment that wasn't discussed, because we'd already decided, and it was normal in our minds to continue. We had decided we were going to build a guitar company and that's what we woke up and did each day.

There's something innately respectable about persevering. Working through the challenges of any pursuit is not something anyone wants to do; it's hard, discouraging, and takes a long time with no immediate reward, but it's something that is worthy of respect and admiration.

The Thing About Money

There are so many reasons to work, or to start a business. But let's face it; if you don't make money at it, you eventually have to give up. Everyone's question is, "How long did it take until you made it?" But what they mean is, "made money." They never ask, "How long did it take you to make a guitar that made you feel good?" We all know that the goal of a business has to be to make money. That's what allows us to stay in business. When I talk about the struggles that were so heavy, what I'm talking about is the pressure and failure to make a profit and take home any money so that we could live. And the same goes for the business. A business without profit is a struggling business.

Let's not confuse the inability to make profit in the beginning and the stress and feelings of extreme failure with the exhilaration and total satisfaction that we obtained from knocking down one problem at a time.

I have discovered over the years that people like to hear about the early days of Taylor Guitars and what exactly we were doing to survive. They find inspiration from the story. They understand what I'm talking about. The more subtle parts of my story come later in the company's history, when we began to work from a position of strength and dominance and could afford the luxury of pontificating over which one of several options might pan out better, and why. Some people appreciate those later business lessons and some don't care about them that much, but everyone, it seems, loves to hear about the beginning: the struggle.

I read adventure and survival books; it's a great interest of mine. Survival stories usually don't come with subheaders like "Adapt to Varying Conditions" followed by an explanation about how they applied that truth—for example, how it came into play on the day their sailboat tipped upside down in the Arctic waters, and they were stuck up to their shoulders in freezing water and had to figure out how to get their EPIRP deployed. Survival stories are self-evident and readers devour them even though they already know that the storyteller survived, because he lived to write the book. Knowing the ending doesn't ruin the story. It's the story itself that intrigues people.

Making Decisions

We made some good decisions and a big factor in all of our decisions has always been to choose the option that would help us create a future. Sometimes Kurt and I had different ideas about whether a decision was good for our future, and we discussed them. We are both very good at putting our points of view out on the table. Often he has better insight than I do, and sometimes it's the other way around. Most often, though, we agree and can see the sense in the same thing.

As an example, I wouldn't advocate operating without business insurance, but I remember the day when Kurt and I asked ourselves what in the world we were insuring? We were insuring nothing, so we canceled our major loss insurance and anything that wasn't straight liability and saved the money. It was money we didn't have to spend. People were shocked. How could we be so irresponsible to risk the loss? We weren't shocked, we were broke, and we thought it was a brilliant decision to cancel our insurance and be able to save the money to tell the tale later. I'm telling it now. When we also decided to re-entertain Rothchild's offer, it wasn't an issue where I felt vindicated that Kurt finally came around to this decision; rather, the time had simply become right for us to proceed with them. We were in a dire situation, plain and simple. It wasn't the time to hold on to our individual ideas unless we could get some guitars sold to make those ideas legitimate. Without the sales, it's all just talk. I don't know if we would have made it another few months without that decision. We probably would have, somehow, but it was the right decision to make in December of 1976. Kurt and I both felt the same way.

At that time, the guitar business was pretty good. Martin Guitars, founded in 1833, was near their all-time high production to that date of nearly 20,000 guitars per year, or roughly 80 guitars per day, compared to the one per day that I was starting to achieve. Gibson, Guild, Mossman, Gurian, and a half dozen other brands were all available in stores.

These guitar companies made us feel like we were always a day late in entering a music store. We'd arrive to show our guitars and the store would have just committed to one of these other lines and used up their money. Rothchild distributed two other brands of great acoustic guitars: Larrivée Guitars and Augostino Guitars. Their job was to add expert sales and marketing to our line of guitars in order to compensate for our lack of brand recognition.

Store owners loved our guitars. They were always impressed at how easy our guitars were to play and how accurate the intonation— the guitar's ability to play pleasing chord forms that sounded in tune—was. One store owner even said, "The only thing wrong with this guitar is that it doesn't say 'Martin' on it." He didn't buy any Taylors that day. But there were other stores who pioneered our line, taking the time to show guitar players what a Taylor guitar was all about.

We worked out an agreement with Rothchild, and I'd like to tell you that things got better right away, but they didn't. First of all, they did not pay the same price we'd been charging dealers for our guitars, as they had initially indicated. By the time we'd made our deal, the retail price climbed ever so slightly, but the price that we received to build a guitar decreased by one-third. We actually signed a deal where we received less money per guitar in the hopes of selling more and being able to concentrate on making them, rather than having to spend energy getting the sales ourselves.

On February 17, 1977, we made our first delivery to Rothchild of only 10 guitars, and two more guitars to our old dealers. After that, every guitar we made went to Rothchild. We shipped 11 guitars in March and 5 in April. Counting 9 guitars we had shipped to dealers in January before signing the Rothchild deal, we shipped 36 guitars in the first four months of 1977, which was no better than our 1976 shipments, except that we received one-third less money per guitar. We kept thinking that we might not have shipped anything at all if we hadn't signed up with Rothschild, and we were still hoping to increase sales as we got used to this new relationship. And we did; we shipped 21 guitars in May, 38 in June, and 32 in July. By the end of the year, we'd shipped 257 guitars. More guitars than 1976, for less money, but over 250 new people owned a Taylor guitar and we were alive to tell the story. Now we could say that over 500 people were playing a Taylor guitar and we thought that would help us turn a corner. We also hoped that the next year would bring more steady business while we worked on our production costs.

I say we "shipped this many guitars" like they appeared magically—as if the guitars were lying around just waiting to be shipped. But we had to actually build each one of those guitars. Even though I'd made a few hundred guitars by then, at 22 years of age, I still barely knew what I was doing. Even though my mind was preoccupied with sales and money pressure, my days were filled with making guitars. I spent my time trying to figure out the nuances, the forces at play, the craftsmanship required, and the tricky business of it all. It was, and is, about the guitar, which is a lifetime pursuit, but it is also about the factory, the methods, the tools and fixtures, and the whole craft of making that guitar. I simply could not design a guitar without thinking about how I was going to make it—and then make it again, so that it was easier and better than the last time.

In those first few months, our only models were in the 800 series. Almost immediately, we added the 900 series, which was more expensive. Rothchild took our guitars on the road, calling on guitar stores around the county, and we got instant exposure. But price was an issue, and Rothchild wanted less expensive models, so we also designed the 700 series, which sold for a bit less than the 800s.

Hard Work and Dedication

We were pretty regimented in our early years. Work started every day at 7 A.M., and we didn't allow ourselves, or each other, to be late. We were also very aware of how much each one of us contributed to the workload because we kept time cards. People who knew us thought it was funny that we worked for ourselves, that we were our own bosses, and yet we were so strict about the hours we worked. I'd see the ads on TV about how to "Be your own Boss" how to "Enjoy the freedom of working for yourself." I especially loved, "Make all the money you want." I would always laugh when they came on, and continued to do so for years to come.

We'd have bouts of being critical of one another, in which we'd challenge each other regarding tardiness or not working hard enough. Then we'd add up the hours worked and see who was putting forth the most effort, each one of us trying to defend our own position and situation. The tension of being financially broke would manifest itself in these little disagreements. But we kept coming back to work and sticking with it regardless.

We also didn't believe in getting sick. You could forget that excuse. The only thing we were able to count back then were the hours worked toward a goal, and the number of presumably good decisions we made. We didn't have any market share, any earth-shattering ideas, or any product that customers were beating the door down to get. We did have bills to pay and guitars that were behind schedule, and our only assets most of the time were our bodies and our willingness to work, so we worked—day in, day out.

Rothchild was eager to take on the delivery of these guitars. They had several sales reps out in the field and the first shipments of guitars from Taylor went mostly as samples to them. With all the different instruments they were selling, they had a substantial investment in salesman samples and we thought they must be pretty rich to afford it. By May, we had to hire and train enough new employees to maintain higher levels of production coming off our line.

We hired employees from the high school in our neighborhood. I'd call the wood shop and metal shop teachers and have them send me their best seniors. We hired some pretty talented kids who seemed to like this first job of theirs. It was also the only way I could figure to get employees that were younger than me. I was a good craftsman and not too bad of a leader, but the thought of employing someone who was 25 or 30 years old, when I was just turning 22 myself didn't appeal to me. We did end up hiring some guys who were older than me by more than a few years and I had to be their boss even though I was young, didn't get paid, was borderline homeless, and had holes in my clothes.

I came in one Saturday and found an employee standing in a pile of broken sets of rosewood sides. He was bending sides to get ahead for the week to come. He couldn't figure out why he kept breaking the sides, so he just kept going through the only material we had to make guitars. He broke about 15 of the 30 sets of rosewood sides we had purchased for our higher-end guitars. That was a tough one for me. We bought that wood from Martin Guitars and were delinquent on the bill even before he broke them.

Our First Paycheck

About the time all this was going on, I got engaged to Cindy Rich and we'd planned our wedding for June 25, 1977. We were shipping guitars and I had become tired of the fact that we never got paid. It was one thing to be broke and single but quite another story as I thought about getting married. I was still living with my sister at the time, and would occasionally stay with my good friends, Steve and Marla. I also spent many a night sleeping in my van in front of the shop. I lived on Campbell's tomato soup for 17 cents a can, and liverwurst sandwiches. It was cheap food and it kept me going.

We were buying supplies from a handful of vendors. We'd buy wood, tuners, mother-of-pearl shell, precut pearl inlays, precut abalone rosette arcs, strings, insurance, and electricity, among other things, and I began to notice that those vendors and our employees got paid regularly. That bugged me because I didn't get paid, and we were in the middle of our third year. In fact, we didn't even consider paying ourselves. I started thinking that if we kept this up we'd never get paid. I thought that we were developing a habit, a bad habit, of thinking that someday we'd have extra money and then we would suddenly be able to pay ourselves. I was afraid that day would never come unless we wrote it into the plan.

Of course, paying ourselves and making a profit were two different matters, but it was the idea, and the habit, with which I was concerned. I knew if we were not profitable, then anything we paid to ourselves would just be a draw against our equity in the business. Making a profit was essential, and if we were not doing that, then we had to improve and find a way to achieve profit. But of equal importance was to take another step toward strengthening the business enough to pay its expenses, and the owners' salaries were certainly a legitimate expense.

I sat down with Steve and Kurt and said that I had noticed that not only did we not pay ourselves, but we had ceased to even discuss it as a possibility; we had developed a habit of not including that in our business perspectives. I told them I was beginning to realize that a certain amount of business was actually being handled successfully and that we needed to work ourselves into the plan, as well. I wanted us to get paid, and I had reached a point where I was willing to consider paying us first as a concept. Then, if we didn't actually have the money, I wanted to analyze all those things that we could pay instead. I suggested we could stop buying things that stood in the way of us getting paid. I reemphasized that the amount of the pay wasn't as important to me at this time as the priority and regularity of the pay.

I began to ask myself why I would pay employees and not myself? I could do my work for free and then do their work for pay. I'd work more hours if needed. The same thing went for vendors. Why pay someone else to make an inlay for my guitar? That's kind of like giving my job away. I didn't care if each of us had to work 15 hours a day to make up for the loss; we had to change things so that some of the money that was flowing through our hands would be able to stay in our hands.

Kurt agreed with the concept, got excited about looking at it that way, and went to work on planning for it. We sat down and came up with a figure that we could pay ourselves and that we felt comfortable with no matter what went wrong. The amount was $15 per week. There you have it. Fifteen dollars.

I was satisfied. That would buy some gas and I could count on it. Kurt and I felt that there was a gradient to achieving goals, so every week on Friday we got a paycheck, and every week we got a pay raise. The raise was $5 per week. That meant that the first week, I made $15; the second week, I made $20; the third week, $25; and by the end of the first month my salary was $30 per week and rising. I felt good, like I was finally on my way. We applied that scheme for several weeks and eventually stopped the increases at $85 per week and were content at that pay rate for well over a year.

With that salary and the $9,500 per year that Cindy was earning as a first-year schoolteacher, she and I bought a little shack of a house, in Lemon Grove, just a few blocks from the shop—for $16,500, including the furniture. It was only 600 square feet, and I couldn't stand up in the bathroom because the ceiling was too low. The walls were separate from the foundation and weeds had worked their way into the bathroom. Still, we were excited. I moved in and she joined me the day we got married.

Improving our Craft

In June 1977, we were gearing up for our big industry conference, the NAMM (National Association of Music Merchants) show, which was being held in Atlanta, Georgia, that year. I was nominated to attend. With all the guitar makers that would be there, the guys in the shop wanted me to find the answers to some of our remaining guitar-building questions. It was going to be my first major event where I could see what other people were doing.

I took a red-eye flight and arrived in Atlanta early in the morning. I'd never traveled that far on my own before and it seemed so exotic and important. When I got to the hotel, I fell upon the bed and conked out so deeply that when Ed Rothchild phoned me to tell me when and where to meet, I just mumbled "okay" and hung up the phone. When I woke up later, I remembered him telling me vital information but I had no idea what that information was. Thankfully, I managed to find my way to the floor of the show and meet up with them.

I arrived at the Rothchild booth to see our guitars displayed and was pretty impressed. Right next to them were the Larrivée guitars, and I couldn't believe how well designed they were. It made me feel like I had a long way to go in order to call myself a guitar maker. Then I met Jean Larrivée, and we became instant friends.

It was at this show that Jean told me about fretting a guitar after the neck was on the body. I can't say that any one person taught me how to make guitars, but I can say that there were certain people who influenced me. One suggestion here and there, and I could take it the rest of the way.

I had been making guitars for a few years when I noticed that sometimes the necks would turn out good and sometimes they wouldn't. The bad ones were only noticeable after the guitar was completed. To fix them, we had to remove the frets from the fingerboards, sand them so that they were level, and re-fret them. It would look wonderful, except that it was very hard to fret fingerboards while the necks were attached to the bodies; the frets would bounce and chatter when you hammered them into the fret board. It was also difficult to get the ends of the frets to stay down. Fretting the neck after it was on the body seemed like a good concept, but I couldn't figure out how to hammer the frets in neatly until Jean showed me all the secrets, including the correct fret wire to use, which I had to order directly from Holland.

That interaction is my most prominent memory from the Atlanta show, because I mentally checked out after discovering this new technique. All I wanted to do was get home and apply the idea. There is one more thing I remember from that show: I had to leave early to fly home and get married. On the night I left on another red-eye, there was a party at Rothchild's hospitality suite in the Hilton. I mingled, obviously being just a kid and a newcomer. I remember hovering around Jean who was talking to Stuart Mossman, a pretty successful guitar maker at the time, who'd just signed a deal with Conn Musical Instruments, where they began distributing his guitars. Everywhere I looked I saw Mossman guitars, because he'd made it to the top from where I was standing. He was making about eight guitars per day at the time, which seemed unattainable to me. He was chatting about the guitar business with Jean, and was talking about his "million-dollar company." I couldn't believe my ears. A million-dollar company? I was in the presence of gods! I got a ride to the airport, went home and got married, and Cindy joined me in our little house.

I don't remember what happened sales-wise at that show, but we must have gotten a little shot in the arm. Again, I mostly remember the new guitar construction ideas I'd learned while away. Following the show, I worked on improving our efficiency every week. It was sometime in the fall that I finished a run of model 855 12-strings. Just before starting this batch, I had made a drill jig to predrill the tuner hole screws on the back of the peghead. This would save time and help line up the tuners.

When it came time to affix the tuners onto the guitars, I opened the boxes to find that they'd changed the design of the tuners to have only one tab. I had drilled two holes in my guitars. That meant another lot of guitars rendered useless. We called everywhere and couldn't find tuners. Out of desperation, I called Jean Larrivée, up in Canada, and asked if he might have some mini tuners. He said that he was just finishing a batch of 12-strings and he'd check the tuners he had for them. He called me back and said that the tuners were what I needed and that he'd send them down that day. I said, "What about your guitars? Don't you need them for those?" I was thinking he might need to ship guitars just as urgently as me. He answered by saying, "Don't worry about that, eh? The important thing is to get you guys going."

We only got $385 for an 855-model guitar when we sold them to Rothchild. Even in the late 1970s, that was not very much money. That was our flagship guitar, the most expensive standard model we made. That model retails for over $4,000 today.

8 Figuring It Out, One Guitar at a Time

We'd been doing business with Rothchild for just under a year and we were getting used to hearing not-so-good news from them. The thing with new products on the market is that sell-through at the retail level is the whole game and evidently, our guitars just weren't selling through. There are certainly a lot of reasons for that, but the biggest reason was that people hadn't heard of us. A small percentage of our stores had great salespeople who believed in our guitars, and they did a great job of showing them and sending happy customers home with Taylors, but most stores expected customers to simply walk in and ask for Taylor guitars. As it turns out, both strategies are important. We needed to market to the consumer, and the store needed to show the guitar and make the sale.

At the time, we thought selling the guitars was now Rothchild's job; therefore, it was their problem. But as it turned out, it was actually our problem. This is because they had other guitars they could sell if our guitars were too hard to move. They made agreements with a lot of suppliers and they could sell whatever was easiest. But since we'd signed an exclusive agreement with them, we were unable to sell our guitars through any other channels.

For a year, we'd enjoyed what we called, "filling the pipeline." Rothchild ordered enough guitars to stock their warehouse, provide samples to their sales reps, and to ship to the stores who decided to carry Taylor guitars. But unless some of those guitars sold through to customers, our business would eventually come to a halt. We, and Rothchild, had done well selling the guitars into stores, but we hadn't yet learned how to get the guitars to reach the customers.

We made it through that year but the production process was still not working the way we planned. We now had six people working for us trying to get our production done on time. We were attempting to make 12 guitars per week, working 10 hours per day, four days per week. That gave me time alone in the shop on Friday and Saturday to design new tools and catch up on work. We were never able to complete those 12 guitars per week. We always fell short, and couldn't figure out why. In fact, we only completed about two-thirds of that amount because we shipped 399 guitars in 1978, which averages to about eight per week.

When the Summer NAMM (National Association of Music Merchants) Show of 1978 rolled around, I shared a room with fellow luthier, Augie Loprinzi. We had quite a time together. After the show, I flew to New Jersey with him. Not only did I get to see his shop, but he took me down to the C.F. Martin Guitars factory—the oldest guitar company in the United States. It was awe inspiring.

At his shop, Augie had some very interesting jigs and fixtures, which I went home, built, and implemented in our shop. But more than that, he taught me the one thing that changed the production of our guitars forever. We were talking about production flow and the fact that I was having difficulty getting my guitars done on time. He explained how he made his guitars "one at a time," so to speak. In other words, every day he'd set up jigs and make the parts he needed for that guitar that day. I argued to him that it was more efficient to set up the jigs once and make all the parts for a batch at that time—heck, even to make enough for six months. I told him how we made our guitars 10 or 12 at a time to take advantage of the setup times. He cross-examined me and got me to admit that we never actually finished those batches of guitars on time. How did he know that?

Augie asked me, "Bob, which would you rather have, one done guitar or 10 half-done guitars?"

It only took a moment for me to get the idea. It infiltrated my thinking to such an extent that it's hard to explain. I immediately recognized this idea as being a way to help solve everything from cash flow to training new craftsmen. I would be able to go home and make guitars every day rather than every week. This became the backbone of the production at Taylor Guitars.

One complete, or 10 half-complete guitars? Which would I rather have? I wanted a finished guitar, shipped and invoiced. I didn't want half-done guitars; they meant nothing to me. They vacuumed money out of my pocket. I wanted a faster return on less investment so I could then repeat the process. I wanted cash flow. I wanted steady work and income, rather than the never-ending ups and downs. I could apply this principle to anything. It led me to think of all the half-done projects in my working life. What if I could rewind, and recover all the energy and resources that were wasted on half-done projects? I could not wait to get home and align my life and work to this notion. I felt like a magnet being instantly spun around to point north. In larger companies, they have more developed approaches, known as *just in time* or *lean manufacturing*, but my understanding of it was almost primal in nature. I owned the idea and applied it as though I was the first person to ever understand it.

Everyone is exposed to some truth, some solution to the puzzle, some overarching concept that could change their working lives, or some idea that they could make their own in order to drive a lifetime of fruitful work habits and improvements. That is the role that this particular principle assumed in my life. Since then, I've had other guitar shop owners ask for advice and I tell them about this, but I haven't seen anyone take the bait. They're looking for something else, usually a faster, more convenient solution, like a new machine or technique. People are intrigued by the concept but can argue their way out of its blessings without much trouble.

That was the good part of the trip. The next part was not so great. Well, at least a portion of the next part. Aside from manufacturing guitars, Martin Guitars also operated a sawmill and would sell wood to guitar makers. Upon his return from NAMM, Augie had to drive down to the Martin factory to pick up some wood.

He'd been to their factory many times over the years and had a relationship where he could just walk in the back door and help himself. We also bought wood from Martin.

We walked in and Augie disappeared to do some business, so he parked me at a corner of the factory where I saw the most incredible sight of my life. This was a real guitar factory, steeped in time and tradition with real men making guitars. They weren't a bunch of scraggly hippies like we were. They had haircuts and wore aprons, with pencils and rulers in the pocket. Their benches were clean and organized. You could eat off their floors and the smell of wood permeated the whole place. I walked away from my designated spot to peek around the corner, where I glimpsed guitar making like I'd never seen before. I saw wonders that made my head spin. I thought to myself, "I could make my factory look like this someday." All I was seeing was a small section of their factory, but it was enough. Any more might have been lethal to my young mind. I'd already been hit with a flash of mental lightning from what Augie asked the day before, and I didn't need more. I was full. I needed to implement.

I felt so unbelievably lucky to be a part of this industry. For years after that day, I would have dreams about being on my own walking through that factory and looking at the guitars being built. But on that particular day, I was jolted from my dream when Augie introduced me to the fellow in charge of the wood division and he said, "Taylor Guitars? Hey, when are you going to pay us for the wood we sent you months ago?"

I was so embarrassed I thought I'd die right there. I thought that evaporation would be a good way to go. It sort of ruined the rest of my time with Augie, because I was sure that he thought I was a bum. He didn't, of course, but I felt like one. I didn't know whether to offer excuses as we drove, or just not talk about it. I did a little of both. I felt like such a loser. The invoice was for about $1,200 and after a year they sent us notice that they'd written it off. They didn't badger us at all about it; they just wrote it off. We did finally pay that bill to Martin.

About six months after receiving the notice, we saved enough money to pay them, and Kurt sent in a check. Geez, I hated those times.

There was another bill that we paid after a long time. For some reason, American Airlines sent us a check for about $500. We were so broke that it was in the bank covering bad checks before we could even find out what it was for. As it turned out, they had double paid us for a damage claim. Kurt kept that on the books as a bill payable and a couple years later we sent them the money with an explanation as to what it was for. We felt good about ourselves, but they were too big to notice, of course. I think we were hoping to get on the Merv Griffin show or something: "Ladies and Gentlemen, please welcome Kurt Listug, the man who paid back $500 to a huge corporation who accidently gave them money and didn't know it." But we just went out to the shop and made guitars instead.

A New Mind Set

I heard it said once that anyone could do good work, given enough time, but a good craftsman does excellent work very fast. I came home from that NAMM show and my visit with Augie and couldn't wait to get started on this new method of building guitars. This was a concept, which to me was more powerful than something specific. To be successful, specific actions must be applied to a concept, but still, this excited me more than any machine or fixture I'd devised up to that point. What I understood from this concept was that I would keep my work cycles short—the shorter the better—and try to get a return on my investment more often. It was allowing me for the first time to get my mind wrapped around this writhing octopus-like thing we were calling a guitar shop. Since we had almost no working capital, we committed ourselves to do what the idea suggested.

Our employees were still working four days per week, Tuesday through Friday, while we worked six or seven days per week. We would work on 10 or 12 guitars in a batch and work until that batch was completed. We penciled in the date when the batch would be finished but it still didn't seem to go quite like we had planned. Things would bottleneck here or there, or get waylaid along the way. An operation could be done wrong, perhaps a router set too deep, or we'd anticipate a part to be a certain size, like the tuners I mentioned earlier, and if we made that mistake on one guitar, we made it on all 10 or 12. We'd discover our mistakes much later, of course, because it was only once every week that we might do a particular operation.

To implement what I learned, I decided that we had enough manpower to make three guitars per day, and I quit thinking about what we made in a week or a month and only focused on what we made in a day. We divided up the work into the departments and created schedules. By now I had thought of all the benefits of this daily cycle and how the myth of the set up times could be handled. I know I talked about one guitar at a time, but the real concept is getting guitars ready to sell each workday. In our case, the number of guitars we could complete in a day was three. Nobody would ever do this, but can you imagine if I started a batch of 5,000 guitars and everyone worked on them until they were done and shipped? What if the whole company worked on bending the sides and then eventually all met in the warehouse and packed those guitars for shipping a couple weeks later? Ridiculous, you say? Then why wouldn't it be ridiculous to do that at three guitars per day? Spreading out the workload, and doing nearly every operation on a daily basis, works. A person can even work alone and be lean. If I worked alone, I'd make one guitar, say, every week. But if it took three weeks for me to be able to do every step because glue or lacquer was drying, I'd start a new guitar each Monday and write a schedule so that once a week, a guitar was completed. This is similar to what you might see in a cooking show. They mix the cake batter and put it in the oven, and immediately pull out a baked cake that they'd put in the oven earlier. That's how I wanted to make guitars.

In order to accomplish this, I'd need to make three complete necks per day. I had an idea of how long each operation would take so I wrote down each step and then put the estimated times next to the procedure. If I wasn't sure about the time required for a step, I'd simply do it in my head, like a gymnast going over her routine in her mind while waiting for her turn on the sidelines. I've made guitar parts like that many times in my head. I just start a stopwatch and do the job mentally, and when I'm done imagining the work, I record the time. It's pretty accurate for things that take less than five minutes. Longer operations I knew from experience, or I'd time myself actually doing it, or even guess. Once the schedule was done, I added the time up and divided it by 10— the number of hours we worked in a day back then. That number gave me the amount of people necessary to get the job done, theoretically. I learned over the years that if I didn't like that number then I'd just go back and cheat a little here and a little there. That's one way we reduced the amount of time it took to complete some of our operations; we just allowed less time. We pushed ourselves and each other to work better and faster.

If glue dried instantly, we could have made three necks in a day, the same day. This not being the case, the work had to be stretched out over several days. So there was a production cycle for each part of the guitar, and the parts that were made simultaneously had to have enough manpower to ensure that we had equal numbers of each part ready to be assembled every day. It requires more people to make three bodies per day than to make three necks, so maybe the body department has three people while the neck department has one. If you saw me make necks back then, it would resemble a cooking show. I'd work on cutting and shaping parts until I glued them together. Then, I'd take parts I had glued yesterday "out of the oven" and just continue the process in a very linear fashion. Each day, I would start three new necks and complete three I had started the day before.

My next job was to convince my employees that this new strategy made sense. It was very difficult for the guys doing the work to be able to resist their strong desire to put three fret boards through the slotting process and stop at only three boards. They just had a natural desire to slot a lot of fret boards, since they were doing it anyway. But I kept repeating Augie's question: "What would I rather have, one done guitar or 10 half-done guitars?" I had, even then, a strong commitment to this idea and I had no problem doing just the three. They thought I was going overboard. They wanted to convince me that while they were at the machine, they could slot more fret boards for free, essentially. But then what would they do tomorrow at that time to take advantage of the time they supposedly saved today? The answer is that they would do nothing with that time, which led to the unraveling of workday productivity. I spent a lot of energy trying to convince my employees that the idea was sound. It's amazing the resistance one can get even from the people who are supposed to be working for you. The way I saw it was that if we spent any time at all doing anything that wasn't directly related to those three guitars we were trying to complete, then that time was being wasted and we'd never get that time back. We had limited money to see us through until the guitars were sold and so I wanted to convert our work and effort into money in the shortest time span possible, so I could invest the money back into materials for the next guitars.

By using this method, it was easier to determine the working capital needed to make each guitar, because you could calculate the labor, materials, and overhead from the time we started the guitars to when they were finished. It required 22 days at the time for a guitar to travel through the entire cycle. So there were 22 groups of three guitars traveling, each needing working capital. We didn't get paid until 30 days after we shipped, at best, because few dealers felt inclined to pay us on time, since they had their own working capital problems. We were undercapitalized, but we struggled through.

It didn't dawn on me until later that some of our capital was coming from our suppliers, and by paying them late we were actually forcing them to lend us money beyond what they had agreed to do. That's pretty standard in business, but when I realized this particular consequence, we worked hard to clean up our act and become better customers to our suppliers.

The thing that we discovered using this new production method was that every day's work schedule was the same. This constant repetition allowed us to start fresh every day and aim to do better than the day before. It also allowed us to know when each day's work was complete and when it was necessary to stay late in order to finish the day's work. I was learning, on my own, how lean manufacturing worked. This was a necessity, because I was in the manufacturing business.

Practice Makes Perfect

Some people prefer variety in their lives. Some jobs require more variety than others. If you're a baker, you bake—every day. If you're a writer, you write every day. Heck, if you're a thinker, you think every day. And if you're a pop star with hit songs, you sing those same songs quite a bit, if not every day. It's all in how you perceive it. I found the reliability of a consistent schedule to be very satisfying. Each day, I made guitar necks for a portion of the day, because I was done by lunch with that part of my work. I completed every step of the guitar neck-making process, and eventually, I got very good at it. My quality and my quantity improved.

With the production coming off the line more steadily and on time, our profit problem was then a result of our costs. The truth of the matter was that we were in no position to raise our prices, which would have greatly improved our profits, so I focused on bringing our costs down. I felt that the new scheduling method I was using to run the factory was only the beginning and that it would continue to improve. I thought I had a production ethic that would be valid no matter how large the company grew. I was relentless about making guitars in a steady flow. It took years for our staff to fully embrace the new system, but eventually, with steady training and guidance, they understood the benefits of the new process and were able to adapt and maintain the workflow without me policing them.

With constant repetition and some guidance, the employees began to get better and faster at their craft. This was a natural outcome of their efforts.

You Are Only as Good as Your Employees

Labor was our highest expense and it seemed that making guitars faster was the key to making a profit. Not more guitars, just less time. This would prove to be a long, uphill battle. In those days, our costs were high, almost higher than what we were paid for the guitar. I would be called upon to lower our costs and I'd always take the opportunity to put in a good word for us to improve the value of the guitars via marketing and salesmanship. It took years before the cost and the pricing were well matched.

So, my fledgling leaner production method was just one of dozens of things that needed to fall into place, and as I mentioned, it was difficult to train employees. I was a fast guitar builder and getting people to duplicate my speed was impossible during that time. I can clearly remember my work schedule from those days as if it were yesterday.

I would start at 7 A.M. and work until 11:15 A.M. to get three necks made. This included every single step in making a guitar neck and nothing was premade.

I would bandsaw the blanks, plane and slot the fretboards, cut the Taylor logo inlays by hand with a jeweler's saw, inlay the fretboards and pegheads by marking the pearl's location with white pencil and routing the holes with a Dremel tool. I'd shape the blanks, glue them together, and I'd carve the necks by hand—the whole enchilada. That was three necks in just over four hours, or at worst, just under one and a half hours per neck. The frets went in during final assembly, so I didn't count that as part of the neck-making process.

Outfitting the Shop

By September of 1977, just three months after getting married, I was spending most of my free, nonworking hours building machines. Greg Deering and I had become great friends and worked together on our tools and machines. We'd get together and imagine all kinds of machines and fixtures, drawing sketches and trying to simplify the ideas so we could make them easily and cheaply. He was working on ideas for tools to glue banjo resonator rims and backs, and I was working on shaper jigs and some larger machines like buffers and stroke belt sanders. Greg figured out that a go-kart tire would fit into the rim of a banjo resonator and could be used as a cheap pneumatic clamp to glue the three-ply rim. I figured out that a fire hose could clamp neck parts together. We thought we were pretty smart. We would drive together to the Rohr and Convair salvage yards and comb through their junk trying to buy parts and hardware for next to nothing. We'd also make trips to Los Angeles to visit our favorite industrial hardware and surplus yards, talking about tooling ideas the whole way.

These places had a good selection of hard-to-resist junk. But I had to think carefully about my purchases and show some restraint. I started applying my loathing of half-done projects to the stuff I saw at the salvage yard. As I contemplated buying each item, if I sensed that whatever contraption or machine I was envisioning would never truly come to fruition, then I would pass on the cheap parts at the salvage yard. Pretty soon, this became easy.

A local high school began offering night classes in their metal shop. The teacher, Steve Shoemaker, had a love for teaching folks how to work with their hands and how to become machinists and welders.

His shop was great. There were several industrial metal lathes ranging from 9- to 36-inch swings. They were located outside and covered with tarps because they wouldn't fit in the shop. We were able to repair the wobbly 36-inch wheel of my band saw using one of the lathes. Steve had forging and foundry equipment, several vertical and horizontal mills, a huge radial arm drill press and even some hydraulic three-dimensional copy mills. There was also every kind of welding machine, and a pantograph flame-cutting torch that could cut steel sheets into shapes by following patterns that we cut from plywood. Greg and I were delighted to have all of this at our disposal. We arrived at class on the first Tuesday night and stayed for almost three hours, and then went again on Thursday. This lasted for nearly two years, and we became good enough friends with Shoemaker that we occasionally went in during school hours and did some work. Sometimes, I'd stay until 10 o'clock at night— when he'd kick me out—and then I'd go back to my shop and work until midnight.

Using my junior-high and high-school metal shop experience, I was able to make a lot of machines that I simply could not afford to buy at the time. In Los Angeles, I found some wheels for a stroke belt sander for about $220, and then a used three-phase motor for about $100. I scrounged a magnetic starter, and that took care of what I couldn't make for that machine. I bought steel square tubing and angle iron and welded up a nice frame and painted it Dodge Truck Green. Then, I put on the parts I'd bought and completed a stroke sander for about $500, which is still in use in the factory today.

I made buffers, gluing presses, and special clamping fixtures for end blocks and braces, along with a host of other simpler tools. I'd work on the guitars, filling orders and training employees in the daytime, and in the off hours of the day, I'd be making machines and tools so we could improve our efficiency.

I wasn't a workaholic, even though I believe that there is a season in your life where large amounts of work are appropriate. As I was doing all of this work for the company, I was also making all the furniture for Cindy's and my little house. One day, a train pulled up to the end of the street where Taylor Guitars was located and unhooked a boxcar, parking it off on one side of the train tracks. Two fellows from Arkansas came by the next day and slid open the doors, and we all took in the glorious sight of 20,000 board feet of red oak lumber. These two old boys got the idea of cutting this wood in their backyard and railroading it out to Lemon Grove to sell it. The railroad tracks most likely had something to do with the stopping point, but we felt lucky; I couldn't help but buy a whole bunch of that wood, and I got it cheap. Between making guitars and machinery, I managed to fit in a set of bookshelves, a dining room table, a credenza, some end tables, a lighting fixture, and a few other little doodads.

With all that work, I still ate dinner at home every night with my wife and, later, with my kids. I learned how to get in a half-day's work on Thanksgiving morning and be home before anyone knew I was gone. These were my working years.

When our shack of a kitchen needed remodeling, and I had no idea how to make cabinets the proper way, my dad came down from my parents' home in Washington and stayed for a couple weeks to teach me. We denuded the kitchen to the bare walls and designed all new cabinets. I didn't have money at the time for real lumber, so I went to the fencing yard and hand selected redwood fence boards. They were on sale for about 80 cents apiece, which is real cheap wood. I picked the quarter sawn, red heart boards and stickered them up in a pile. With fans blowing on them, they were dry in two weeks, and ready to go by the time my dad arrived.

That lumber made a beautiful set of kitchen cabinets. We also made a hutch with leaded stained glass doors, corner cabinets with lazy Susan shelves, and built-in spice racks, among other small conveniences. My adorable, poverty-stricken, wife-of-a-guitar-maker had the best kitchen of all our friends, and that's the truth.

This handyman phase of my life lasted years. Sometimes, I literally stayed up all night working on those projects and actually saw the sunrise the next day before I quit to go to work and start making guitars again. I still have a workshop of my own today where I build furniture and work on my Hummers and Land Cruisers. The point is, I make stuff—a lot.

By the time 1978 rolled around, we were making about three guitars a day, and learning that we couldn't get employees trained to a point where we got guitars finished in few enough hours to be profitable. My daily schedule was working well; it was just populated with too many workers for the amount of guitars we were producing. We knew we were on the right track with our plans, but we kept searching for more to learn, trying to crack all the codes to achieve financial success. Our only two possibilities to increase profit would be to lower our cost, or raise our price. Raising the price simply wasn't an option yet.

Our guitars were coming off the line more steadily and my convictions about how to go about producing them never wavered. I began focusing increasingly on the training of employees, and on helping them to achieve the best results possible by coupling their skill sets with my tools and fixtures. Kurt learned accounting. He has a natural talent for it and gained additional expertise each year. He learned that a manufacturer should make a gross profit margin of at least 40 percent, so we worked on accomplishing that each quarter.

I've known a lot of business men and women in my life and we all seem to have a different understanding of what profit margins represent. Just to clarify, when I say a 40 percent gross profit margin, I mean that our cost of manufacturing should not exceed 60 percent of the sale. For us, that meant our materials, overhead, and labor combined should be no more than $600 if we sold a guitar for $1,000. The other $400 is there for sales and administrative expenses and if we only spent $300 of that we'd have a net profit of 10 percent. These figures were survival percentages, in our estimation, and to be prosperous, we'd need to beat them. On the gross profit end, the materials and overhead were pretty stable. My job was to get the labor dollars down, and I failed quite consistently at this task in those days.

It's Business, Not Personal

There came a point when we ran out of money, finding ourselves in crisis mode again; we weren't sure what to do. We were still paying off the money we'd originally borrowed to start the company, plus additional money that we'd borrowed in the years that followed. Things were looking bleak, and one day it occurred to me to take a loan on my house. I mentioned it to Kurt and Steve and it sounded good to them. I figured that I could borrow about $7,000, which would give us a big shot in the arm. I wasn't interested in loaning the money to the company; I was interested in investing the money. I borrowed the money and put $7,000 into Taylor Guitars and got a small percentage of each of Kurt and Steve's shares for it.

The sun rose and set, and we worked in the factory—hiring, training, negotiating, and facing bad news. The end of 1978 came and we were beginning to consider what life would be like without Rothchild involved in our affairs. While we were busy making machines, perfecting our skills and building guitars, Rothchild was failing to purchase the number of guitars they'd agreed to buy. Again, to be fair, dealers were not experiencing the sell-through that all of us wanted to see. We were broke, but at least we got our $85 a week, and I was happy about that, even though oftentimes we couldn't cash the checks.

Trying to breathe new life into the relationship with Rothchild, we brainstormed with them on new models. They would always suggest that less expensive guitars would sell better. We responded with designing the 500 series guitar. The 510 was a mahogany dreadnought with spruce top, rosewood fretboard and bridge, black binding, and a two-ring rosette. We figured that the lower material cost, the black binding, and the two-ring rosette would save us enough money to sell the finished product for less. Plus, we thought selling these would be better than selling nothing, so we agreed to it.

The reality is that we were fooling ourselves. To think that putting in two plastic rings around the sound hole of a guitar rather than three would save us money was ridiculous.

Any guitar, no matter how simple it is in construction, takes as much time and resources as any other. These guitars still had to go through nearly every process that the 810 went through. We probably saved an hour of labor and $20 in materials when we made a 510. We only paid ourselves $1.75 per hour, so the labor savings didn't change anything. By then, I had made more tooling to save time, and we worked hard and fast. I applied my belief that quantity was every bit as important as quality when it came to being successful. Still, we sold those guitars to Rothchild for $150. I don't know how we did it, but we did. We just put our heads down and plowed through. Kurt required Rothchild to place a large order for these new, affordable guitars, and he also required them to prepay 50 percent of the invoice for the first 100 guitars or so. This gave us an infusion of cash—$7,500 to be exact—and helped us to stay afloat.

We shipped the first model 510 to Rothchild on October 13, 1978, just two days before our fourth anniversary. We billed them the $150 for the guitar and then half of that went against their prepaid credit account, so we received $75 income for that guitar. That was a tough realization, and the result is that we got tougher on ourselves. I loved guitars, but in a way a cowboy loves his horse; he might share his apple with the horse, but he doesn't kiss it. He rides it and thumps it on the head if it gives him grief, and they journey through life together, the best of friends.

I never thought about quitting, but I did fear going out of business. The thought of being forced out of business against my will horrified me. We were locked into this relationship with Rothchild, and I was beginning to think it would be the death of us. We were making and selling guitars, but we received no money for our labor. Then it hit me that it might be better for Rothchild to go out of business than for us. Were they going to ask me to make them a $25 model next to make it easier for them to sell?

January came, and I drove up to Anaheim, California, for the NAMM show. I got there hours before Kurt and Steve. Rothchild's booth was looking forlorn and a bit depressing. Things were not going well for them in general, not just with us. Larrivée had already split with Rothchild, and Agostino had gone, as well. Their booth just spoke of failure to me that year, and something clicked in my head that it was finally okay for us to end our arrangement and leave them. That would be hard because we had contracts, and I'd made friends with them. In fact, I was terrified at the thought of telling them I wanted to leave the relationship.

They had trouble selling our stuff and we couldn't do anything to help ourselves because of the exclusive arrangement we had with them. We were being killed by the dying host. That was just not acceptable to me, and so I decided I wanted to be on my own, where I could make or break my own future. I called Kurt on the phone and said that I was ready to leave Rothchild. He was a bit surprised but was all ears. I told him how I thought the whole scene looked like a losing proposition. Kurt was ready, or got ready fast, and agreed with me. He came to the show and saw the situation for himself, and I think he delivered the news to Paul right there at the show. As usual, we filled Steve in on our decisions and he went along after a bit of argument.

Kurt did most of our negotiating when it came to banks, real estate, marketing, and sales. He's a planner and his resolve about things is as strong or stronger than mine. But we have always respected and supported each other. When it came to making decisions, we got on the same page pretty quickly, either by actually feeling the same way, or by swinging to the other's point of view, or by compromise. We have always depended on each other for information. Kurt was in charge of sales, and was responsible for building our brand, but he respected my opinion and when I arrived at NAMM and relayed to him what I saw and thought, he was not only ready to listen, but he would have called me and said the same thing if he were there first. Once I made my report and said I was willing to break away from Rothchild, he put it into second gear, got himself ready, and had the tough talk with Paul. He did the work.

Paul was shocked and felt betrayed by our decision, but we stuck to our guns. The show was a bummer and I don't remember much from it. Even if we didn't sell as many guitars on our own, we'd be better off because we'd be receiving 50 percent more money than we'd been receiving while selling through a distributor, who resold to dealers, who then finally sold to an actual guitar player. We did make a slight profit those two years with Rothchild. Being a partnership at the time, all the profit went onto our personal income tax returns. My $85 a week salary wasn't being covered by profits and once again, we ate into our equity in the company. My tax return shows I earned $3,470 in 1977. My 1978 return shows that I made $1,140. There's not enough money in guitar making for all the people involved in the process to make a profit along the way.

After the show, we flew to San Francisco and had a big supplier and distributor summit meeting with all the people who were still doing business with Rothchild. They begged us to stay, but we declined.

We shipped our last guitar to Rothchild on January 27, 1979. That month, we sent them 69 guitars for a total billing of $12,901, of which we received one-half due to the fact that we were using up their prepayment credit account. So, 69 guitars shipped and $6,450.50 came in from that. I was relieved to be done with the Rothchild-partnership portion of my life. I liken the experience to doing wind sprints, uphill in the sand, with heavy chains dragging behind you. You can build some muscle doing that, but it's tough work. We learned a lot and we made some market progress through it all, as Rothchild exposed new dealers around the country to our brand of guitars, but it felt good that we were once again going to be in charge of our own destiny.

9 Finding Our Place

Rothchild dumped the remaining guitars they had in stock at fire-sale prices and the dealers snapped them up, making it difficult for us to sell those dealers any new guitars. Rothchild was closing up shop, so they needed to rid themselves of their inventory—not just ours, but the other brands they distributed, too. In February of 1979, we shipped only 12 guitars to dealers, but in March, we shipped 56 and in April, we shipped 38 guitars.

Kurt worked hard to maintain good relationships with the dealers we worked with at the time. That relationship with Rothchild cost us in the short term, but through our time spent working them, we gained a dealer network that we wouldn't have had the where-withal to achieve on our own. Without Rothchild operating as our distributor, and instead selling directly to the dealers, we received 50 percent more money on each guitar we built, and we had more control over our production. So we returned to making and selling higher priced models, rather than the cheaper 500 series that RMI demanded.

I had my first realization of the true meaning of working capital and how it affected a business during this time. We were trying to make more guitars than we had the working capital to support. Even though Kurt was doing a good job selling guitars for the first several months of 1979, we were still struggling to make ends meet. He was only one person and he had to juggle his role in sales along with shop responsibilities, plus the burden of managing the finances. Later that year, sales began to fall, because even though he was a stronger salesman, Rothchild had six people on the road selling guitars. Their manpower was an obvious advantage.

I began to discuss with Kurt the possibility that we were trying to be a larger company than we had the money to become. I drew a slightly absurd analogy to make my point: If the city of San Diego was going to build a new convention center, a guy who builds patios on the weekends isn't qualified to bid on it. He doesn't have enough financial power to undertake such a task. Maybe that same patio builder could stretch himself to the max and bid on building an entire house, if it wasn't too large, but there is a limit to the types of projects in which he is able to participate.

Thinking in the extreme, like this, can help a person understand that there is a point where something can work and a point where it can't; we fit somewhere along that scale. Even if we were making a few more guitars than we could afford, as long as we recognized and admitted it, then we could correct it. We decided that we were, indeed, making more guitars than we could fund *and* sell.

We decided we had reached a point where we had to lay off every one of our employees if we wanted to keep the business going. Once again, our company consisted of us three partners. Painful as it was for us to break the news to everyone that their jobs with us were over, they accepted the reality of it and understood. Being that this was the first job for most of them, we all moved on very quickly. We squared up with them, they went on their way, and we started over once again. But we weren't starting from scratch, as we now had some level of sales, a small dealer network, a few years of experience, a tiny reputation, some work in progress, and a lot more knowledge than the day we started almost five years earlier. We were even writing ourselves modest paychecks each week, even though sometimes, again, we couldn't cash those checks.

The decision to let our staff go was one of the best decisions we made that year because it took so much strain off of our limited working capital.

In 1978, we built and sold 449 guitars with 11 of us in the company. By contrast, with just three of us, we managed to make and sell 399 guitars in 1979. Though that was 50 less guitars, it meant I was a faster guitar builder than our employees, and if we were going to have people working with us, we would have to make to the process of performing high-quality work faster and simpler for employees. I didn't know exactly how that would be achieved, but it would involve tools, methods, and training. During this phase, I gained confidence in our abilities and reset my expectations for the next time we'd hire people. I began to rethink how I would train a person, what I would accept as a minimum amount of work to accomplish each day, what schedule we would operate on, and how I would choose the right people. I knew I had to improve my ability to hire the right people and be a strong leader and manager. I knew the day would come when we'd hire again.

We were able to make that number of guitars that year, because there were some partially completed guitars left on the shelves after reducing our production numbers. We exploited the situation by completing more guitars in that one year than we would be able to do if we'd started from scratch.

Kurt made guitar bodies, and he was a trooper because his natural skill isn't guitar making or working in a shop, but he was serious about letting me teach him, and he did good work. After he would finish his production work, he'd work on sales and accounting, and to make things fair, I was assigned a list of dealers who I had to call and sell to. We still designated Fridays as the day to do non-production work, but that never seemed to happen for me. Steve did a good job applying finish on the guitars; the only catch is that he'd often complete a week's worth of polished bodies and necks on Thursday instead of each day, so guitars that should have been assembled a little at a time throughout the week had to be assembled at the last minute. I'd stay up all Thursday night gluing on bridges and necks, so that we could complete those guitars on Friday, when they were supposed to be completed. Many of them shipped that same day. He was often behind and it caused the rest of us to work erratic schedules. Our plan to make a steady flow of guitars each day would get as far as the finish department and then pile up into batches.

Notwithstanding the erratic schedule, it felt great doing the work ourselves, without any employees. It allowed me to concentrate on being a craftsman and make a clean, sharp guitar. I loved high-quality craftsmanship and could always tell the difference between good and mediocre work. I was usually dissatisfied with our final product and would work on my techniques or my tools to improve the quality. I could see clearly what could be done better on the guitars. I also had a natural desire to produce a substantial quantity of guitars. I've always felt that quantity was as important as quality. If we do incredible marketing, we have to make that legitimate by making enough guitars to fill the demand. Increasing market share means making the guitars, not just marketing them.

People view things differently when it comes to the size or focus of a company. There are some guitar makers who prefer to work alone and make a couple dozen guitars a year, each one being made to near perfection and tailored to make a select few clients happy, rather than worrying about market share. Everyone needs to find his or her own place within the business realm. For each person who believes running a factory is how you become a success, there is a person who finds success by working alone. For every actor who wants to make a blockbuster, there is one who wants to excel in small theater productions. Some chefs want to cook for an elite clientele and others want to see their recipes go nationwide.

I enjoyed growing my company and making more guitars.

The secret is to know how you feel and what you want to achieve, and then to work hard to make it a reality. Each model has its own drawbacks and rewards. Some excellent craftsmen prefer to make a single guitar, one at a time, and then find a buyer. They can work in a garage-size workshop, literally having little or no overhead and making a decent living pretty soon after starting their businesses if they do good work. They don't have to split the money with dealers, and as their reputation improves they can command higher prices. These people often become the close personal friends of famous performers. They are truly connected to their clientele, which is enviable.

But the drawback is that they work alone, and if they don't work, they don't get paid. If they don't have the proper facilities or machinery, they breathe wood dust and finishing fumes, which often affects their health. If they injure a shoulder on vacation or while working, or cut a tendon with their chisel, they're out of work until they heal.

If you want to grow your business, you must be able to pay your employees, landlords, the retailers, the magazines' advertising departments, and the government's payroll taxes. This typically means experiencing years of expenses that stand in the way of making a profit. But there comes a time (or at least, there is the potential for the time to come) when the company itself is strong and can support you or allow you to take time away from the workbench to explore new products and ideas. And it can support others in the company in the same way. It's much different than working alone, but both have their advantages.

Trying to keep a leg in each camp is difficult. It's difficult to have both popularity and exclusivity at the same time. That doesn't mean that Taylor Guitars are not highly regarded; we're just not exclusive.

At 25 years of age, in 1979, I was well on my way to operating a factory that makes very good guitars, while many of the guitar makers I knew at the time felt that what I was doing was not the way to make high-quality guitars. They felt that being small, by default, was better for the guitar. I understood that, but I also understood the beauty of being a larger company, so to me, it wasn't a stretch to imagine making a large quantity of good-quality guitars. Our dealers appreciated what we did and liked having our guitars available to their clients, and they liked the fact that we were willing and eager to make more.

I may have been eager to make more guitars at that time, but my desire outweighed our ability to actually *sell* more guitars. And one of the reasons for that was that the musical times were changing. When we started Taylor Guitars, the acoustic guitar market was at its peak. It had grown steadily for a couple decades, but by the early 1980s, it had fallen off to nearly nothing.

The Rise of the Electric Guitar

Martin Guitar Company, which reigned supreme, had already been in business for 131 years in 1974, when we started our little company. In the eight years from 1974 to 1982, Martin went from total production of more than 20,000 guitars to about 3,000 guitars. Their company was going through one of the most trying times in its history. In many ways, the fact that they survived is more remarkable than the fact that we survived. Reducing a business by that much and living to tell the tale is an amazing feat in itself.

Saturday Night Fever was playing in the movie theaters. Disco music became the craze, 1980s rock was coming alive, and nobody was playing acoustic guitars on albums or when performing this new genre of music. These mainstream music shifts continued to stifle our growth, but in hindsight, it might have also been one of the biggest contributors to our success.

I think about what would have become of us if there had not been this incredible downturn in our industry back then. I was less aware of popular music being the cause of our frailty, and much more aware of our own limitations while we learned our craft and our business. I'm not sure I was cognizant of all of the different factors affecting our business. All we knew was that every day was a struggle, and every day we made a little progress.

Larger companies like Martin Guitars noticed the difference, however. They had plenty of resources and experience to produce and sell great guitars, but the market caused them to shrink beyond their control. Markets do that. It did it to typewriters, and to film cameras, and it did it Martin guitars. It would have done the same

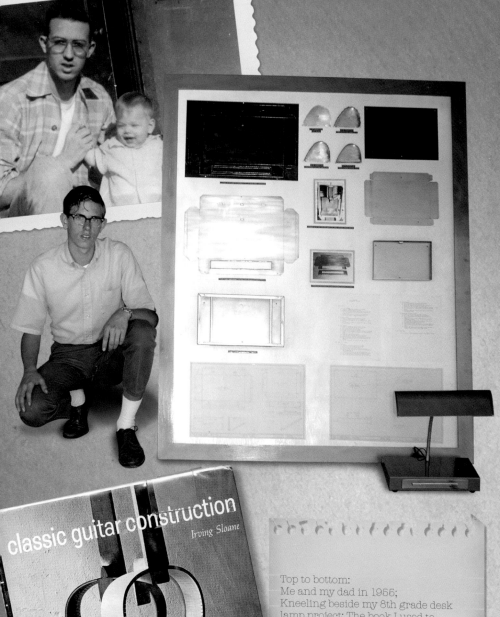

Top to bottom:
Me and my dad in 1955;
Kneeling beside my 8th grade desk
lamp project; The book I used to
construct my first guitar at age 17.

classic guitar construction

Irving Sloane

photographs, and step-by-step instructions

Opposite page, top to bottom:
Banjo neck I made in 12th grade
woodshop. I hand-cut the inlays;
My high school motorcycle; My
banjo-making friends, Greg and
Janet Deering; The first guitar
I built, age 17.

This page, top to bottom:
Cindy, me and Greg camping
in the desert, 1979; The jeweler's vise
I made in junior high school;
My second guitar, made in high
school, age 17-18; Me holding early
Taylor guitars, 1976.

office 2804500   Date 4-23 19 74
o. 6474   Dept.
Name Randy Northrup
       College Ave.
Address

QUAN.	DESCRIPTION	PRICE	AMOUNT
1	rosewood dreadnaught		450 00
2	ab top		50 00
3	ab rosette		10 00
4	ab back		20 00
5	ab around f.b on top		20 00
6	ab around head		25 00
7	D-45 inlay		20 00
8	fish on truss nut cover		5 00
9	handle bar bridge		10 00
10	binding on f.b		10 00
11	total		670 00
12	tax		40 20
13			710 20
14			
15			
16			
17			
18			

KEEP THIS SLIP FOR REFERENCE

Customer's Order No.

Redifprm
5H 33

WESTLAND MUSIC CO.
Taylor guitars

Opposite page, top to bottom:
The receipt for one of my first customers,
Randy Northrup; (Front guitar) One
of the first 810 models, 1975; (back
guitar) walnut/spruce dreadnought, 1974; Me sitting in my
new kitchen, with the fenceboard-
made cabinets, 1979; Kurt on top
of his Falcon, admiring his
"kingdom," Westland Music
Company.

This page, top to bottom:
Sanding a bridge; Early bolt-on
neck from 1975; Fretting tool
designed in 1994, now used
by hundreds of guitar
builders; Neil Young in "Rust
Never Sleeps" with his Taylor,
1978. My 1976 810, which I
played in church for 20 years.

This page, top to bottom:
Parts notebook of early employee Eric Vossbrink;
Lemon Grove shop, 1980; Me working on guitars,
1975; Kurt at the sidebender, 1976.

Opposite page, top to bottom:
The entire crew in Lemon Grove, just before we
moved to Santee in 1986. Many of them still work
at Taylor today; $500 loan agreement from my
Grandpa Taylor; Payment schedule for the same
loan. Kurt drew up our documents and has always
been very financially tidy!; My new resaw, used to
saw guitar tops and backs, 1981.

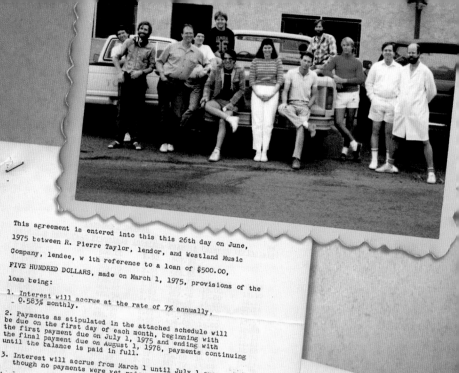

This agreement is entered into this this 26th day on June, 1975 between R. Pierre Taylor, lendor, and Westland Music Company, lendee, w ith reference to a loan of $500.00, FIVE HUNDRED DOLLARS, made on March 1, 1975, provisions of the loan being:

1. Interest will accrue at the rate of 7% annually, 0.583% monthly.

2. Payments as stipulated in the attached schedule will be due on the first day of each month, beginning with the first payment due on July 1, 1975 and ending with the final payment due on Augul 1, 1978, payments continuing until the balance is paid in full.

3. Interest will accrue from March 1 until July 1 even though no payments were yet made.

4. Each monthly payment will include both an interest charge, and a portion of the priciple.

The total finance charge is $68.60.

Dated:

Signed: *R. Pierre Taylor*
R. Pierre Taylor

Robert R. Taylor
Robert Taylor
Westland Music

Schedule

Interest	Balance	Payment	(Principle)	AL
2.92	502.92			
2.93	505.86			
2.95	508.80			
2.97	511.77			
2.90	499.67	15.00—I		
2.83	487.50	15.00	3.23	
2.76	475.26	15.00	12.10	
2.68	462.94	15.00	12.17	
2.61	450.55	15.00	12.24	
2.54	438.09	15.00	12.32	
2.47	425.56	15.00	12.39	
2.39	412.95	15.00	12.46	
2.32	400.27	15.00	12.53	
2.25	387.52	15.00	12.61	
2.17	374.69	15.00	12.68	
2.10	361.79	15.00	12.75	
2.02	348.81	15.00	12.83	
1.95	335.76	15.00	12.90	
1.87	322.63	15.00	12.98	
1.79	309.42	15.00	13.05	
1.72	296.14	15.00	13.13	
1.64	282.78	15.00	13.21	
1.56	269.34	15.00	13.28	
227.22	1.40	255.82	15.00	13.36
213.55	1.33	242.22	15.00	13.44
199.60	1.25	228.55	15.00	13.52
185.97	1.17	214.80	15.00	13.60
172.05	1.08	200.97	15.00	13.67
158.05	1.00	187.05	15.00	13.75
143.97	0.92	173.05	15.00	13.83
129.81	0.84	158.97	15.00	13.92
115.57	0.76	144.81	15.00	14.00
101.24	0.67	130.57	15.00	14.08
86.83	0.59	116.24	15.00	14.16
72.34	0.51	101.83	15.00	14.24
57.76	0.42	87.34	15.00	14.33
43.10	0.34	72.76	15.00	14.41
28.35	0.25	58.10	15.00	14.49
13.52	0.17	43.35	15.00	14.58
	0.08	28.52	15.00	14.66
	13.60	13.60		14.75
				14.83
				13.52

Opposite page, top to bottom:
Cindy's and my first house, not much more than
a shack, 1977; Pregnant Cindy outside the same
house, after I remodeled on nights and weekends,
1981; Kurt walking the plot of our new factory in
Santee, 1986; Santee factory, 5,000 square feet,
coming together; Prince's purple 12-string.

This page, top to bottom:
Our first Fadal brand computerized milling
machine, which changed everything for us; Our
new factory in El Cajon, 1992; The factory layout
I did for El Cajon; Inlay I did for friend and player
Harvey Reid, 1988.

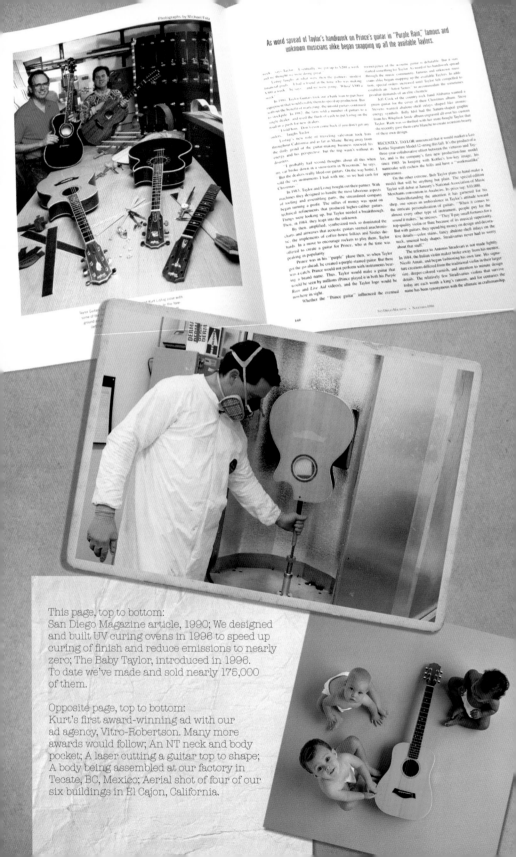

This page, top to bottom:
San Diego Magazine article, 1990; We designed and built UV curing ovens in 1996 to speed up curing of finish and reduce emissions to nearly zero; The Baby Taylor, introduced in 1996. To date we've made and sold nearly 175,000 of them.

Opposite page, top to bottom:
Kurt's first award-winning ad with our ad agency, Vitro-Robertson. Many more awards would follow; An NT neck and body pocket; A laser cutting a guitar top to shape; A body being assembled at our factory in Tecate, BC, Mexico; Aerial shot of four of our six buildings in El Cajon, California.

IN ITS SIMPLEST FORM, A GUITAR IS JUST A HOLLOW BOX MADE OF WOOD. It's UP TO YOU TO DECIDE HOW TO FILL IT.

This page, top to bottom:
Two issues of Wood&Steel, our quarterly publication since 1994; Me and Jason Mraz, fall of 2009; Taylor Swift playing her "glitter guitar" adorned with hundreds of Swarovski crystals, at the launch of her second CD, "Fearless," in 2008. We hosted the launch at our venue.

Opposite page, top to bottom:
Me and Kurt in San Diego Magazine, November 2010; Talking to Taylor Swift on stage at her launch party in 2008; Me and Zac Brown in Iraq, spring of 2010, on a Zac Brown Band USO Tour.

MADE IN SAN DIEGO

THEY'RE HOMEGROWN, BUT THEIR REACH EXTENDS FAR OUTSIDE OUR COUNTY LINES. SOME OF OUR FAVORITE HOMETOWN COMPANIES PRODUCE PRODUCTS WE LOVE, FROM BEER AND SPORTS EQUIPMENT TO SATELLITES AND ANTIBIOTICS. CHECK OUT 11 COOL SAN DIEGO BUSINESSES.

BY ERIN CHAMBERS SMITH, ADAM ELDER, DAVE GOOD, BRANDON HERNÁNDEZ AND MIKE SENESE
PHOTOGRAPHS BY JAMES MACIARIELLO

Custom Grand Symphony with master-grade
Hawaiian koa, Florentine cutaway, abalone rosette,
rosewood binding, and "tropical vine" fretboard inlay.

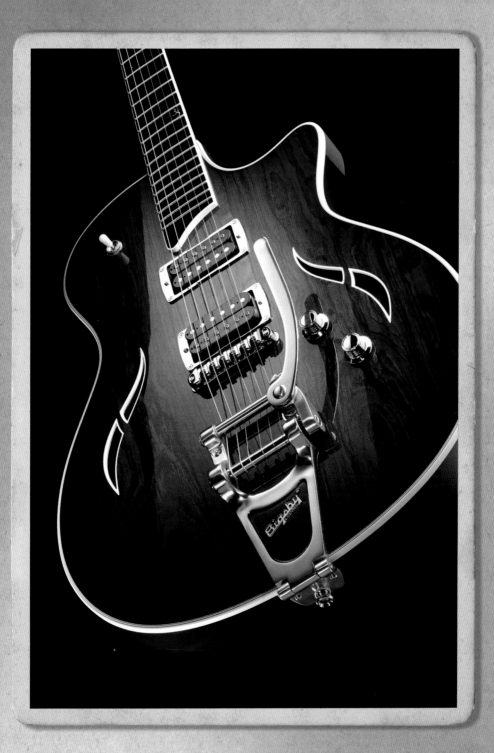

A 35th Anniversary T3/B with a cocobolo top, sapele body, and two HD humbuckers with coil-splitting capability.

Our 900 Series guitar peghead with mother-of-pearl
inlay and Gotoh tuners.

to us, if we had something to lose at the time. When we started, Martin Guitars was a hundred times larger than us, but as the 1980s progressed, they were only two or three times larger than us. It was not because of our incredible growth, but rather because the market shrunk them down to nearly our size. This leveled the playing field a bit, making us a contender with our dealers.

At this same time, Gibson Guitars also experienced an incredible lull, nearly going out of business between the years 1974 and 1984. There were changes in ownership and plant location that stopped or nearly stopped their acoustic guitar production. And the other great American acoustic guitar builder, Guild Guitars, was suffering not only from ownership changes, but also from the folk era decline—so much so, in fact, that solid body electric guitars became the main focus of their production in the 1980s; they gave very little attention to their acoustic guitars. It was a rough time for everyone!

Even my good friend, Jean Larrivée, quit making acoustic guitars during these years and made only solid body electric guitars just to survive.

Meanwhile, in Lemon Grove, California, every moment of every day we were fighting the same fight we started the day we began our business in 1974. We only knew one thing, and that was the struggle to make and sell acoustic guitars. We could catch glimpses of slow progress toward our goal, while others were either putting their acoustic guitar making on the back burner, or experiencing a downturn of 80 percent of their production. With each guitar we sold we were encouraged, and we saw this as growth. By contrast, other companies had already experienced success and were accustomed to it, so it must have been tougher for them than for us.

If the market had been great, and if corporate conglomerates hadn't purchased and mismanaged Gibson and Guild during our fledgling years, perhaps the three of them would have squelched us; perhaps dealers would have seen no need to carry our guitars.

I'm not saying that our success is because disco music shrank the competition's business, but what was happening in the industry is absolutely part of the story. It's important to acknowledge the parts of a success story that are not of your own doing. When people fail, they love to talk about all the things they had no control over to account for their failure, so the successful person is obligated to do the same.

The dealers loved our guitars. They are guitar enthusiasts at heart and they loved the shape and feel of our guitar necks, the brilliant and balanced tone, and our craftsmanship. They bought guitars because they wanted to, and thankfully, they kept acoustic guitar playing alive during those years, no matter how unpopular it had become.

On the Road

By the end of 1980, our sales became difficult to come by yet again. The success we had the year before, making and selling 399 guitars, wasn't going to happen. We knew we were capable of making guitars, at least, but we just couldn't sell them. So in 1980, we made only 100 guitars and carried inventory from the previous year into the new year. We finally leveled out at about 300 guitars per year with three or four people working.

In June of 1980, we drove to the NAMM show in Chicago, Illinois, where we exhibited as Taylor Guitars for the first time. We rented a U-Haul trailer, hitched it to my 1978 Volvo, and transported a display I'd made, along with 12 guitars, from San Diego to Chicago without stopping. It took 52 hours of driving with no hotels, since we couldn't afford any. We arrived, located our booth space, and discovered two four-foot diameter concrete poles in the middle of our 10-by-20 booth, which required that I hack up our display to fit around them. We were across the aisle from a 1980s rock-inspired electric guitar company called Dean

Guitars, who were extremely popular at the time. We proceeded to spend four days watching them sell guitars like hotcakes, while we experienced nothing other than hearing people walk by and commenting that they thought we made good guitars. The end of the show netted the sale of our eight sample guitars, plus six orders. That's it!

The 52 hours driving home, after such a disappointment, was much harder than the 52 hours out, filled with anticipation.

We made a couple of good moves early in the 1980s, though. It seems that we were always blessed with at least one dealer who was a real champion of our guitars at each point of our business development. There was Fred Walecki who began carrying our guitars right from the start, and in the early 1980s, there was Arnold and Morgan Music in Dallas. They bought our booth samples at that year's NAMM, and they sold more guitars than anyone at the time.

They loved a deal, so when they bought our samples it was under the conditions of an extra discount. We agreed. They flat out told us once, "Hey boys, you need us more than we need you." And then they'd wait for us to become desperate enough to offer them a deal. They'd order guitars on a regular basis, paying normal prices, but it was the bulk purchasing opportunities for which they waited. By the time summer was over, we had a surplus of 100 unsold guitars back home, so Kurt and I called Arnold and Morgan to make a deal. We gave them a huge discount off the price, and they took all 100 guitars. We took in some cash with the deal, about enough to recover our costs, but rather than pay bills with it, we decided to fund Kurt's travel costs to sell guitars. We thought that was our only chance. Thinking that it was do or die, if we could sell guitars we could work our way out of our hole.

We put Kurt in his car and sent him out. I told him there was no need for him to return, because if he couldn't find some new dealers interested in carrying our guitars, there would be no business to come back home to. He totally agreed, and I didn't see him much during the next year or two. He traveled and called on stores, simply cold-calling, walking in and showing them our samples. The dealers liked the guitars. Kurt learned how to ask for the order and the combination of the two resulted in orders. Not an overabundance of them, but enough to sustain us. We'd talk on the phone. He spent holidays in a Holiday Inn, and watch the San Diego Chargers play on a hotel TV. At least once, he parked his car, long term, and flew home to do some accounting, and then he flew back and resumed his road trip. He honed his skills. There are a lot of independent music stores that can recall the times when Kurt would call on them, building the Taylor Guitars name.

And Then There Were Two

In the early 1980s, we worked every day to refine our skills, streamline our processes, and resolve problems we were having. With Kurt on the road, I had to hire an employee when Kurt left, so this was the third time I made the attempt to be an employer. It seemed to work this time. We got a lot of work done, except that Steve and I still had differences about how we each worked, which we were unable to resolve.

While mine and Kurt's roles were easy to define, the role of our third partner, Steve, was growing harder to define. Kurt was advancing in his skill as an accountant, financial planner, and salesman. I was becoming excellent at building the guitar, managing the workflow, and overseeing the factory. We both advanced in our areas on our own, without anyone telling us to do so. Steve's role was less defined, because he didn't gravitate strongly to any one aspect of the company. Problems that come from within a business are worse than those that come from without. Internal problems can drain the energy out of a person. So, we began to think of how the company would operate if Steve were no longer a part of it. I was constantly torn between the stress of enforcing the removal of one of the partners from the business, and then thinking that eventually he'd find his place and we'd all make this business successful. Then, I'd circle around to thinking it's no use and that we'll never get anywhere if we don't decide one way or the other. The pressure of this decision was overwhelming.

By contrast, the challenge of guitar making, and building our market share and our sales volume seemed much easier. I could expend limitless energy toward that goal. It didn't make me tired or give me feelings of giving up, like those feelings of despair that ate at me regarding Steve and what we needed to do about our poor alliance. Kurt and I would talk about it over the phone and when he came home, we explained to Steve that our time together was coming to an end. Fortunately, Kurt had the sense on our first day to start our business with a good partnership agreement that included a buy-sell agreement, which spelled out how to invoke a buy-out and what the price would be. We bought Steve's shares and Taylor Guitars became a two-man partnership.

That was March of 1983. The next day, Kurt and I realized that since I had bought a couple shares with my house loan a few years previous, that I owned 52 percent of the business to his 48 percent. We agreed we wanted to be 50/50 partners, so we adjusted for that and have never looked back.

We doubled our business the year we bought Steve out. Just how much a conflict from within can negatively affect the outcome is immeasurable. We doubled our business the following year, and again the year after that. We've been growing ever since.

It was 1982—eight years had passed since we started Taylor Guitars. Every day, we learned a little bit more about how to make our guitars and run our small business. Our production had been erratic, as were our sales, causing our financial health to teeter on the brink, like a patient almost ready for hospice. On the bright side, our quality was improving steadily and so was the knowledge of our brand. The outside world wasn't aware of our financial hardships, and to them we were becoming viable as a guitar option. We had resolved our internal issues by severing our partnership with Steve and purchasing his shares. At the same time, we sensed the possibility of a change in our market and we felt poised to take advantage—and take advantage, we did.

10 Gaining Traction

The day after resolving a looming issue is always better than the day before, and so it was for Kurt and me when we finished our buyout of Steve's shares. We felt free to maneuver, so we took that energy and ran with it.

The 1980s were filled with more of the same stories I've told before—struggling to pay bills, obtain enough sales, and run the factory with any kind of mastery. But in 1983, the first year with just Kurt and me as owners, we doubled our business and achieved gross sales of over $200,000. We'd been on a $100,000 plateau for the previous three years. The second year on our own, we grew to $450,000 in gross sales, and have been growing ever since.

We celebrated our tenth anniversary in 1984 with the confidence that we had figured out how to make guitars well, but with the sobering knowledge that we were still in the most depressed market our industry had seen in decades. Every day of my life was spent trying to improve our guitar-making skills, while Kurt was dividing his time between sales and finance, with the majority of this time being spent on selling.

One day, in 1985, one of our dealers, McCabe's Guitar Shop, called Kurt and told him that they wanted to purchase a special guitar. This wasn't the first time someone had asked for something custom, but this order was different; they wanted us to make them something unique, or unusual, and they didn't care what it was, or how untraditional it turned out. They asked us to surprise them.

By this time, the business had grown and we again needed to hire people to help us build guitars and manage the company. We had hired a dozen employees, and being an employer was working out a bit better than before. We were older and we had learned from some of the mistakes we had made in the past. I'd hired a local craftsman named Larry Breedlove, who had become a skilled instrument builder by building banjos with Greg Deering. Larry was also an artist and sculptor, using wood as his primary medium. Larry and I worked well together, enjoying the same kind of design and approach to building guitars. It was a nice combination of talent, certainly enhancing our company's overall ability to offer great guitars.

For guitar enthusiasts, he is the same Larry Breedlove who left Taylor Guitars to start his own company in the 1990s. After a couple years, Larry's feelings about business ownership changed and he left Breedlove Guitars to return to Taylor. There is as much of Larry's design influence in a Taylor Guitar as there is from me. Breedlove Guitars' third owner is currently running the company that Larry founded.

Kurt, Larry, and I discussed the McCabe's Guitar Shop commission and Larry brought up the idea of using watercolors on wood. He'd been working on an art project, having nothing to do with guitars. He'd figured out a technique that allowed him to paint wood in a mosaic-type design, but with sharp edges so the colors wouldn't bleed onto one another. We wondered what McCabe's would think of a painted guitar with multicolored flames around the sound hole, all on a background color of blue or red.

Our thinking was that not only were we in the middle of the acoustic guitar doldrums, but with disco and 1980s rock ruling the airwaves and the fashion sense of the day, people had begun to associate acoustic guitars with folkies, hippies, and old fogies. This is not good when you own an acoustic guitar company!

There was certainly a loyal group of musicians who were committed to their acoustic guitars and were playing at coffeehouses or performing small acoustic concerts here and there, but the mainstream didn't even think of putting an acoustic in their act on the stage. Acoustic guitars weren't being brought into studios when artists were recording their albums, either. Even country music had relegated the acoustic guitar to a prop that nobody really played seriously on stage. These were the days when bands like KISS, Motley Crew, Poison, Styx, and Van Halen ruled the scene. Even the electric guitars had morphed into designs that looked like axes, weapons, or spaceships. The good old electric guitar models like Gibson's Les Paul, or Fender's Stratocaster, seemed outdated compared to the models that the bands at the top of the charts were playing. The bands were costumed and their guitars were dressed up, as well.

We hoped this new design would help make the acoustic guitar more hip, cool, and apt to be picked up and played by a Top-40 artist.

Meanwhile, we had teamed up with two very talented acoustic guitar performers, one named Chris Proctor and the other named Harvey Reid, who were traveling a circuit playing colleges and small venues filled with acoustic guitar enthusiasts. In fact, they were on the forefront of the new finger-style acoustic guitar music that was gaining popularity among players and listeners. They could always draw a crowd of 50 to 200 people. They made their own records and sold them at concerts, and figured out how to make a living playing their guitars.

Kurt, Harvey, and Chris theorized that since Chris and Harvey were on the road anyway, playing small venues, that they would certainly be near one of our dealers and perhaps we could combine resources to promote Taylor Guitars at the dealership by having them hold free concerts, or workshops as we liked to call them. We would split their fee with the dealer, but the fees were affordable because their travel expenses were already absorbed by the fact that they were there anyway, probably driving right by on their way to the next college a couple towns away. This filled in the blank days in their schedule and put several hundred more dollars in their pockets each week. Promotion of the events was done via the store's mailing list, and with local press releases advertizing a free concert and clinic sponsored by Taylor Guitars, the local dealer, and featuring Chris or Harvey. The events always brought in customers and made the local newspapers.

Our customers came to hear the music they loved, and learned a bit more about Taylor and what we had to offer. The dealers got people coming into their stores and sold some guitars. Everyone was winning with this grassroots marketing effort, and Taylor Guitars became a little better known.

Harvey and Chris were our stars. We did a lot for each other. We also had a wonderful association with another artist named Dan Crary, who had made a name for himself in the bluegrass and flat-picking genre. Dan, Kurt, and I met and became friends, which resulted in a guitar model bearing his name. He did occasional workshops, and we now had a trio of accomplished artists playing our guitars, a group of dealers who championed our guitars, and customers who trusted in our brand enough to spend their money and go home with a guitar of which their friends might not have heard.

Although we were still making more guitars than we were selling, this new marketing strategy helped sell many of the guitars we were making at the time, which probably amounted to 15 guitars per week. We'd begun working on a five-day production week, completing three guitars per day.

But if we wanted to grow our business further, we needed the world to change. We needed the acoustic guitar to become more popular. We needed to hear musicians playing acoustic guitar on the radio. We needed to run into a friend who knew a song with an acoustic guitar in it. We needed KISS to play an acoustic—like *that* was going to happen. Until acoustic music came back, we figured we'd adapt, and since fashion trends were influencing the style of the instrument, we were willing to adapt. The electric guitars at the time boasted exotic shapes and wild paint, and beneath all the decoration, they were still good instruments. What if we took our good guitars and simply changed how they looked?

We felt we had a lot already going for us in that our guitars were very easy for any electric guitarist to play, and this was becoming a well-known fact to dealers and artists. In addition, we had been designing and installing electronic pickups into the guitars so that a player could plug the guitar directly into the sound system rather than position a microphone in front of the sound hole. Nobody in a large arena show was about to stand with his guitar in front of a microphone, and strum to 10,000 screaming fans. Our guitars were already suited for the task because we'd been working diligently with the manufacturers of these pickup systems for several years. Even our acoustic players like Chris, Harvey, and Dan were pioneering the use of pickups in front of a purist audience. Even though they sat and performed, they still wanted a bigger sound than a microphone could provide.

Larry finished the guitar he designed for McCabe's, and it was beautiful. It wasn't painted, but rather carefully stained with colors that allowed the wood to show through. As acoustic guitar makers, we were proud for it to bear our name. We had something that could compete with the highly stylized electric guitars and costumes on a stage, but still be a real guitar, and not a prop that was made solely for its cosmetic appeal. After a moment of wondering what they were looking at, the owners of McCabe's ended up liking it. The design was more dramatic than they may have expected, but they did ask for something unique.

Prince bought one. It was purple. He knows a real guitar when he sees one.

When that guitar showed up in his video for "Raspberry Beret," which received tremendous airplay, I felt much like I did that day I watched Neil Young play his Taylor 12-string in the movie *Rust Never Sleeps,* eight years earlier. Like Neil Young's guitar, Prince's purple guitar was also a 12-string. Prince was incredibly popular that year, propelled by hit after hit, plus the release of his very successful movie, *Purple Rain*. I never met either of these artists, and they wouldn't know me if I sat next to them on a jury, but they each bought a guitar of ours and helped us get a step closer to our goals.

Kurt had a good relationship with a dealer who sold guitars to Prince and who had been involved with some custom guitars that Prince owned. He had a feeling Prince might buy such a guitar if we made it, but the way it would work is that we would make the guitar on speculation and then the guitar would simply be presented to him, and whatever happened would happen. We weren't in a position to give free guitars to stars and so it was a risk. What if he liked it but wanted it for free? We didn't know, we thought we'd cross that bridge when we came to it. Each guitar and the money it was worth were precious to us. What if he didn't even take notice of it? We'd never made a guitar with the hope that one certain individual would buy it. There was also another catch: Prince refused to play any guitar with the guitar maker's brand or logo on it. I didn't know the reason; I could only guess, but those were the rules. So we made this spectacular guitar, in all its purpleness, with no Taylor name inlaid on the headstock, and had the dealer show it to Prince on the chance he would appreciate it and use it. It all worked out, and everyone knew it was a Taylor even without the name.

During Prince's reign, country music was fighting its way back and the group Alabama was at the top of the charts, probably selling as many albums and garnering as many dedicated fans as Prince. We got to know Jeff Cook, the guitarist of Alabama. Jeff took a shine to that purple guitar of Prince's. Even country acts were playing primarily electric guitars that were colorful and looked cool from the stage. That year, Jeff asked for one in green and used it on stage and on the cover of their best-selling Christmas album.

So there we were with two of the largest acts in the music industry both playing Taylor guitars. At one end of our marketing and promotion spectrum, we had our clinicians doing workshops at dealerships and truthfully, probably producing more sales from that effort than the superstars at the other end of the spectrum. But the superstars did their part. Prince and Jeff, and others who bought those cool colored guitars helped other stars and artists decide that perhaps they were missing out and that they, too, could put an acoustic guitar into their show. Magazines and newspapers, being celebrity driven, couldn't seem to write an article about us without mentioning the topic. Sure they were interested in our guitar-making business, but they also wanted half that time to be talking about Prince or Jeff. All of these elements combined to help revive the acoustic guitar for casual players, producers, songwriters, and the general population.

Right around the same time, MTV went "Unplugged," and that meant that bands had to come on TV and play acoustic versions of their hit songs. The ironic thing about an unplugged show is that you must plug in, and since our guitars were nearly always made with built-in pickups, they were easily amplified on the set. Plus, those electric players loved our guitar necks. MTV's contribution was so impactful that nearly every person alive in the free world knows that the word *unplugged* means "acoustic." It also means "cool." It was beginning to appear that the acoustic guitar was making a comeback. It wasn't long before a song or two on every rock album was an acoustic ballad.

Some say you have to be in the right place at the right time in order to succeed. I think there is a lot of truth to that, but sometimes you might have to remain in the wrong place for a long time in order for your opportunity to present itself. Some people like to define luck as when preparation meets opportunity. You hear the story about someone who goes on a picnic and finds a gold ring in the sand. Then there is the guy who buys a metal detector and looks for gold in the sand and eventually finds it. They truly are both in the right place at the right time when they find that gold, but the guy with the metal detector will probably find several gold rings over time, and might even gain intuition as to where to look for them.

I have to confess that it irks me when people, especially journalists, suggest that they hear it all changed when Prince played a purple guitar. As much as I appreciate that moment, it wasn't a turning point. It *was* a highlight, to be sure, and the market effect was profound even though hard to measure. The fact that a journalist would ask about it is proof of how powerful it was. But marketing has to be turned into reality, and in the business world, reality includes a lot more than simply being known or associated with celebrity. It helped us gain some traction and in our own little way, it helped us to alter the world of guitars. Every successful person I know names a turning point that is entirely different for them than what the public views as the turning point. To the person becoming successful, the turning point is usually something mental—a moment in time, a flash, or a revelation— that allows them to think and act differently.

In the background of what we did to market and sell guitars were other equally important events. There came a time when something happened to change the way Kurt thought about selling, and we would all reap the benefit. Once this took place, Taylor Guitars would never be the same.

11 On the Move

The days were hot in our little shop in Lemon Grove with the south-facing wall that radiated the solar buildup hour after hour. I learned to work at a pace that was just shy of sweat running down my face. I was used to it. The shop was divided into three sections: milling of rough lumber, assembly of bodies and necks, and finishing. I'd spent 11 years of my life working in this 25' × 60' space. It was home to me, and I had rearranged it at least five times over the years. No matter how many times I did, it never got larger; it was always 1,500 square feet.

Right across the driveway was another building that was 400 square feet, owned by the same landlord. We decided to rent it out and build a little office, a rack to hold finished guitars in cases, a packing and shipping corner, and the workbench where we put the strings on the guitar as the final act before bringing it to life.

Kurt worked in that office, which was air-conditioned, and I split my time between both buildings. We had hired a staff of 10 people by then, and were producing four guitars each day. It was 1985 and it had been 6 years since our split with Rothchild. Sales were still scarce so more often than not, we completed our guitars before we actually had orders for them, and Kurt would spend his time on the phone trying to sell them to dealers. Many times we had as many as 50 guitars stuffed in that little room. Our goal was to have no guitars in that room; we wanted to sell every guitar. Any guitars that were in there were unsold. But we continued to make them each day, hoping to get orders.

In the center of the workshop was a whiteboard where Kurt wrote our production schedule, so we knew what to make each day. It was filled out about three weeks in advance and each week was divided into days. Next to the days were written the model numbers we were to produce. It looked something like this: Mon 4/19: 615, 810, 810, 710; Tue 4/20: 855, 710, 715, 610. If a particular model was preordered by a dealer, it appeared in black. If it had no order, no place to go, it was written in red.

Nearly every guitar on the production schedule was written in red, with 45 or 50 more completed red guitars lined up in the room across the driveway. We were making guitars that had nowhere to go.

One day, Kurt came in and erased a red 615 with his thumb and replaced it in black. Everyone looked up as he walked out and headed back over to his office. Later that day, he came in and erased a red 810 and replaced it in black. We couldn't help noticing.

"What's up? You sell a guitar?"

"Yep, sold a couple."

"Wow, way to go!"

Kurt sold a couple stock guitars, and then took orders for more of the same and had to come over and change the numbers from red to black on the board. He began to put the name of the dealer beside those black guitars. Over the next few weeks, he would come in often to write on the board. He'd walk in with a smirk, and like a magician just before performing the climax of his act, he'd wipe sideways with his thumb, erasing a red model number and rewriting it in black. We all began to laugh and soon cheer.

He started coming over five times a day changing the color of the guitars on the board from unsold to sold. We began to anticipate great things when Kurt walked in. It was like we were staging a comeback to win the World Cup. He put on a little show, which went something like this: He'd walk in holding back a smile, erase the red, write the black, and walk out like it was no big deal. No comments, no questions allowed. We were all digging it.

I'm not going to tell you what was going on over at the other building, or what had happened with Kurt, because I honestly don't know. He had figured it out. He had figured it out on his own, like a math problem in school that you don't understand,

and then you get it so you want to do some more, over and over. These first months of steady sales were one of the highlights of our entire business venture. It was as though we'd turned a corner. We had figured out how to make guitars, we were good with our limited money, we'd accumulated some resources, and now Kurt had figured out how to make them sell!

One Friday evening shortly after that, I remember leaving the shop, the sun still shining and warm. I was the last one to go home. The day's guitars were sold and shipped, and all the production was on schedule. I closed the door and noticed that for the first time since we started this business almost 12 years earlier, I felt like I was finished for the day with nothing left to do. I went home feeling free, like I wasn't being held hostage by my dream, but rather, I was living my dream. I'll never forget that feeling, as it was one of the most satisfying feelings I've ever experienced.

Our sales stayed on an upswing, enough for us to decide it was time to think about moving from our little shop to a larger, more suitable place. Kurt began to look around the area and soon found a small industrial park about 10 miles away in the city of Santee, California. With a bit of negotiating, we made a deal with the builder and leased 5,000 square feet of a 15,000 square foot building that was yet to be built. They started on it right away and I began laying out my dream shop. I had a hard time thinking that 5,000 square feet could ever be outgrown, since it was three times the size of our Lemon Grove shop and it had taken us 12 years to establish enough demand to sell three or four guitars a day on a steady basis. Our new shop had the capacity to build 10 or 12 guitars per day. I thought it would probably take another 10 years to achieve that level of production and the sales to support it.

I still had not grasped the difference between increasing what already exists, and starting from nothing. It turned out that increasing was much easier.

I spent the next several months preparing the plans for the new shop, right down to the last outlet and lightbulb. I gave careful consideration to each and every bench, the space between them, and how big they should be for comfort and economy of space.

The new space allowed us to incorporate machines and amenities we could only dream of having in the last shop. I installed a dust collector and much of its ductwork, the spray booth and fan, the air compressor and all the copper lines, the vacuum pump and its lines. I put in the drop ceiling and lighting in the final assembly room and built the workbenches. I built sanding benches that drew the dust away from the craftsman, and then I moved each machine over from the old shop and hooked them up to the dust collection system. We organized the move so that we did not miss a single day of production.

I made my first industrial contractor relationships through that building, using my first electrician and a specialized contractor to install the dust extraction system. I learned how to work effectively with the city's building and fire department and with our Air Pollution Control District. For the first time, I was on the radar of the city because the building was brand new and needed inspections and permits for each stage to go forward. In our first building, we simply did things without asking.

When we moved into the Santee shop, we were making 22 guitars per week. This was the first level of production we'd achieved that allowed for predictable income and profit. It was great to be in our new factory, and Kurt and I immediately started planning for growth. I don't mean we wished for growth, I mean we *planned* for it.

We increased our production at a scheduled rate that he set up in the beginning of the year. Soon we were making five guitars per day and then six. Kurt hired his first outside salesman for the company at about this time. He looked at dealers around the country to see which salesman was selling the most guitars.

T.J. Baden, who had worked for a dealer called Guitar Showcase in San Jose, California, started working for us. Kurt had met T.J., was impressed with his ability, and offered him a job with

Taylor Guitars. T.J. accepted the offer, and the two of them worked together to build our sales. We hit rough spots at six guitars per day, finding difficulty selling that many guitars, but Kurt and T.J. figured it out and got us up to seven and then eight guitars per day.

Sales were going well and production was sometimes challenging with the increased number of employees I had to train. I was still working on the production line, with a daily workload, but I did manage to find the time to train people how to do their jobs. By then I also had some veteran craftsmen who were able to train people in their own departments, and that worked pretty well.

We had made some real progress in our business, but we were still the underdogs—the newcomers—to our industry and had to work hard to keep our guitars in the forefront of our dealers' minds. It often felt like if we closed down and went away, nobody would even notice. Steady production and sales were hard to attain; while the crisis of the early days seemed to have passed, there was still a lot more to do on both ends of the spectrum to get us to a place where we felt like we really owned a piece of the market.

We wanted there to be a noticeable demand for our product, rather than being in a position where we were only able to sell our guitars by pushing relentlessly for it. Truthfully, there was probably serious demand for about half of our production, and the other half is what we worked so hard to attain.

Expansion is hard work and sometimes it involves doing things you never signed up to do. I certainly had an unanticipated project heading my way.

12 Making Our Case

I always wonder about who figured out how to make bread. After you know how, it's simple. You buy some flour and yeast from the store and follow the recipe on the back. I travel in the deserts of the United States, Mexico, and the Sahara, and have learned that staple ingredients don't go stale, like bread does. So I take flour, yeast, salt, and water and make simple pita-style bread that I can bake right smack on the coals of my fire. Just toss it in there like an old paper plate, and flip it over a couple times and let me tell you, it's good. I learned this in the Sahara from shepherds. People have been doing this forever, and yet if I do it for anyone they think I'm a magic man. Well, they should really, because if you think of it, how did the first person learn how to grind wheat and put yeast and water in it to cause it to react, and then how did they think they should put that glob on a fire? How'd they put all those ideas together?

Or how about charcoal? Do the people barbecuing in their back yards know what charcoal is, and how it's made? It's brilliant. You slowly remove the water and the volatile substances from wood in an oxygen-free chamber at a low heat, until what is left is nearly pure carbon. That carbon, or charcoal, burns hot, is easy to light, doesn't smoke like wood, and is lightweight and easy to transport and store. Who figured that out?

I learned how to make charcoal one Christmas vacation in the early 1990s when the fire department informed me, in the wee hours of the morning, that my shop was on fire. When I got there, heart pounding and my stress level at the highest I've ever felt, I found out the fire wasn't in the shop where I made guitars, but rather the shop where I made guitar cases. That was a relief of sorts, because it meant less loss if the whole place was to go up in flames.

When I arrived, the industrial park was flashing red and blue from the rotating lights of every kind of emergency vehicle I could imagine. Firemen were hosing down everything, in a seemingly calm manner as if they'd succeeded in stopping a total loss. I calmed down a lot when I saw that. An alarm brought them to my shop that night, and when they arrived they could tell the building was full of hot smoke that could explode into flames at any moment. With their chainsaws, they went on the roof and cut an 8-foot square hole, which billowed smoke that was dying to get out of that building. Once the smoke was gone, it was safe to pry open doors and enter. In the corner of the building was a machine press, containing a huge block of smoking, black, mess. It was a press used to make the bent sides of guitar cases. I made that press.

The molds in this press were comprised of 24 layers of hard particleboard covered with a rubber heating blanket then a layer of stainless steel sheet. On the way out the door for our annual two-week Christmas shutdown, the operator forgot to turn off the press. It was like leaving your iron on, but much bigger.

The press only heats to 250 degrees Fahrenheit, which is not hot enough to set wood on fire. We use that heat to set the glue that holds the layers of veneer together to form the wooded sides for the guitar cases we build. But in the 10 days that it was left on, it slowly turned this massive four-foot cube of wood into charcoal, which, I now understand, is just how you are supposed to do it, if you want to make some.

Charcoal can light on fire at 250 degrees, so once the wood-to-charcoal conversion was complete, at about the 10-day time, it began to smoke like your barbeque and was ready to light on fire.

I don't know how it feels to lose a business to a catastrophic loss like this, but I know how it feels to drive there thinking that you have lost your business. I'm so fortunate that it turned out okay for us. I was able to rebuild the press, clean up the shop, and get back to business quickly, and without much loss.

We didn't always make guitar cases, but we started one day when we were nearly forced to. The late 1980s found us in our new shop, enjoying how far we'd come. Gone were the setbacks that plagued us early on. Guitars were being built and sold in record numbers for us; nearly eight guitars per day. But there was a new problem that arose and often prevented us from shipping. We couldn't ship our guitars without cases, and we'd receive late deliveries of cases regularly.

When the guitar market shrank in the early 1980s, the factories that made guitar cases suffered. These companies were in places like Brooklyn, New York, and Elkhart, Indiana, and had been in existence for decades. There was infrastructure surrounding them, with suppliers that made musical instrument case plush, and latch hardware. They all began to go out of business about the time we were experiencing good sales and good production for the first time in our history.

The day came when we were being pulled down by their demise. We often had close to 100 guitars waiting to be shipped, and then a partial order of cases would arrive. We'd be dismayed at the awful quality when we would inspect the deliveries, but our only options were to use the poor-quality cases and ship our production, or not ship at all. Calling the supplier and trying to work out quality issues was futile because their businesses were obviously failing. There was one good supplier in Los Angeles, named G&G Cases, who made some acoustic guitar cases, but not in the shapes we needed. Their main business was solid body electric guitar cases. They were able to supply us with a few cases for one of our models.

We began ordering cases from several suppliers, just to get what we needed, but ended up with a mish-mash of case designs. Every supplier's case was different from the others, so there was no continuity in design or quality. Our dealers and customers suffered through, but the whole thing reflected poorly on Taylor. Our customers felt that we should be able to solve this, and they were right.

I determined that the only solution was to make guitar cases ourselves. I began to cut cases apart and learn how they were constructed. They were a formed plywood carcass, lined with foam and plush on the inside, and covered with vinyl and binding on the outside, and held together with hinges and latches that were held in place with rivets. It's very simple construction compared to a guitar but still very labor intensive. The case factories depended on high volume production numbers, and low-wage labor to make their business model work. They lost the volume, and their labor rates continued to climb. Plus they sold to us, and we sold to dealers, and dealers sold to consumers. If I built the case I would be able obtain the higher price that the dealer paid, rather than the price I'd been paying the case factory. Bottom line, I had the ability to sell a case that I made for a higher price than they could sell a case that they made.

We also wouldn't need the high volume production that the case factories needed. This could be viewed as a department of our overall company rather than a company that had to support itself. We got started building a small shop that could produce exactly the quality and quantity we needed. The overhead would be low. I felt that if we could revive the aesthetics and quality of the old-style cases that were made in the heyday of the guitar market, it would help sell our guitars.

I designed the case factory without ever having built a case. Unlike guitars, you can't build a guitar case without using some impressive tooling. All the molds for making the carcass have to be built, along with elaborate glue spreading devices. The interiors of the cases require special glues, made from animal hides, and applied with special machines. We needed riveting machines and big sewing machines that are strong enough to sew through the $\frac{1}{4}''$-thick hard plywood. The day came when we finished building the case factory, and there it sat, empty and gleaming, everything new and unused in a building we rented within walking distance from our Santee factory.

Our friends at G&G Cases were kind enough to support us by showing me their procedures and selling us supplies and materials in the beginning. But I still hadn't made a guitar case and didn't know how to, other than having done it in my head. We had no employees in that factory yet, but some were scheduled to start in a week's time. So on one weekend, my wife Cindy, her mother Patty, and I went to the factory and the three of us figured it out. By the end of a few days we had formed and made carcasses, covered, sewed, and lined them, and put them together with the hardware. We made a batch of 50 cases, and we were on our way. My days of depending on failing case companies were over. Now it was my problem, which was the way I liked it. We began shipping the backlog of formerly case-less guitars and our customers loved the new cases.

We had already gained a reputation for being a company that pressed on, that conquered new territory, that didn't let market conditions beat us back, and amazingly the addition of guitar cases to our factory's production impressed our customers even more than some of our guitar innovations. Our cases fit the guitars perfectly and were made in a style that people loved. Dealers would tell stories of selling our guitars to customers, who were on the fence about their purchase. They'd say, "Do you want to see the case?" Then they'd bring it out and say, "Look at this case. If a company cares so much about their product to make this awesome case, instead of just buying something off the shelf, imagine how good the guitar quality must be, even the parts you don't see inside!"

I've been told by dozens, if not hundreds, of customers, that this story happened to them; that it was the guitar case that sealed the deal on their purchase and was the icing on the cake that caused them to proudly buy their Taylor guitar.

It's complicated enough to run a guitar factory without having to learn to build an entirely new product like a guitar case. But by doing so, we solved a supply problem that was holding back our entire company. On the surface it would be easier to just cope with the supply problem, like the other guitar companies did. They survived the downturn in case production and eventually, cases started being made in Canada as well as China, and guitar makers got cases here and there.

I prefer to look deeper than what is on the surface. We did the hard work, built the factory and learned how to make our own cases, but we didn't just solve a supply problem. We improved the entire package of what the customer bought from us. They were able to buy a Taylor guitar in a Taylor case. The case was branded, and styled so that it was beautiful and recognizable. It wasn't a purchased generic case where "one size fits all," which is another way of saying, "one size fits nothing." They knew that their case was for their guitar, one for every shape we offered, and that translated into them feeling like we made it for them! The dealer's confidence in us rose to a higher degree. The customer's pride in their purchase increased and they loved their case as much as they loved their guitar. Because we showed we cared about the entire product, it had a very positive effect on our business and helped us move to another level. It's like when you buy something from a great retailer and they send you home with your purchase in a branded shopping bag with their store's logo beautifully embossed on the side. You feel good and you want to return to the store.

Taylor Guitars cases paved the way mentally for me to tackle larger jobs in the future. Because it reminded me that once you do the work, you have something that others don't have, and if they want it in order to compete, they have to do that same work. Unfortunately most won't, so if you do, it is noticed.

We began to make more guitars, and with our increased production and the addition of our case factory, our employee base had swelled to nearly 40 people. We were entering a phase where it was time to learn new lessons. This time it was about people.

13 We're All in This Together

Over the years, many fellow guitar makers would visit the Taylor factory to meet our team, take a tour, and perhaps pick up a few ideas they could take back to their own business. One day I was having lunch with a couple of guitar-making friends who stopped by for such a visit. They had a fairly new company where they were making a line of very high-quality, solid body electric guitars. At the time, our production rates were in the neighborhood of about 500 guitars per day. That breaks down to just under 200 high-end guitars made in the El Cajon, California, factory each day, and about 300 less expensive guitars made in our factory right across the border in Tecate, Mexico. There is a lot to see in the El Cajon factory, including several methods of guitar production. Many guitar makers gather inspiration from a close-up visit. During our time together over lunch they began to ask questions of me, knowing that I've been through it all before.

"Where do you get your employees? How are you able to keep your people? Is it hard to find good people? How do you train them? How do you get them to do the work the way you want? Do you have discipline problems? We're having a hard time with some of our long-standing employees. Do you have that problem?"

I'd forgotten. These were the questions I wanted to ask someone every day, it seemed, about 20 years prior. I responded with a question: "So, how many employees do you have now, about 30 or 40?"

"Yeah, almost 40. How did you know?" they asked, a bit surprised.

I knew because that's about the size when things begin to run amuck in a company, and it certainly did for us. By contrast, companies with 5 or 10 employees seem pretty pleasant and manageable. And I have no advice to offer a company with thousands of employees, since I have no experience with that. But I do have experience with having one, a dozen, a hundred, and several hundred employees.

I've read that many people sell their companies once they reach the size where they have about 45 employees. There must be a reason, so I thought about it and looked at my own story to try to understand the trend.

I can't say for sure why most businesses experience this difficulty as their workforce expands. Perhaps this particular problem doesn't occur within law firms or in medical offices. Perhaps they're at each other's throats with only five employees! I joke, but I'm serious, too, in that perhaps *professional* people are educated and focused enough to just do their work and refrain from much of the drama that others experience when it comes to personnel. But I highly doubt it.

I have seen many companies with a dozen or so employees who are very stable and pleasant to be around. But when businesses reach about 40-something employees, there can be problems that you have to witness firsthand to believe.

Most small businesses are started by people with skills who want to make a living working for themselves. Then, as the business grows, they start hiring people to help. But there often comes a point when they are no longer the one building the guitars, or cooking the dinners, or selling to their customers. Instead, they become the manager of all the employees they've hired and trained to do that work.

I've heard it before; a person looks up one day and says, "Hey, all I wanted to do was design and build dune buggies and now I feel like I babysit 35 people all day long. If this is what running a business is all about, I'm selling this thing and getting out."

This is a very common progression within companies when it comes to growth and, subsequently, hiring employees. Think back to hiring your first employee, when you made a point of telling them your vision for the company. You wouldn't give them a job and just say, "Okay, you work over there, and I'll get to you when I can, and don't expect anything but a paycheck out of this." Who would you attract if that was how you communicated? Instead, you might say, "Hey, I like you and I think you and I could work well together. This business of mine looks like it's going to work and I really need some help. I know you can go get a job at a more established place, where there's some benefits and better salary, but they might not care about you, or know your name. If you work for me, we'll work together, and I'll keep it interesting. You can help me build this, and you'll be in on the ground floor. Who knows what it might come to, but there's opportunity here for you if you want it."

When there is a major development or, alternatively, a problem in your company, the few employees you have should be the first to know. Ideally, they would be involved in the good and the bad moments because they're the only ones around. They'd get excited when things went well, because the outcome would have a direct effect on them. And that effect might not even be a financial one, but it would influence their feelings of inclusion and worth.

You'd be in it together.

Being transparent is the right approach when you're starting out, and the situation often dictates that approach. There is no way around being honest and open about the state of the company when your business is struggling to make its way. Whether consciously or unconsciously, you are making a mistake that you'll have to correct in later years when you withhold information from your workers. The mistake is in thinking that you are actually in it together in a way that translates into equal opportunity. Later on in the life of the business, ownership creates opportunities for owners that are not available to nonowners, or employees.

Split Personality

As the owner, you play two roles in your business:

One role is that of an employee, or a worker, someone who should draw a salary for the work you do. In most cases, you start out in your business doing all the work. You consider yourself "chief, cook, and bottle washer," because you do it all. You work alongside those first few people you hire. You often don't even get paid, and you're there on holidays when they're at home having a barbeque.

The other role of your split personality is that of the owner, and at the beginning of a business there is little upside to being the owner. You don't get time off if you're serious about building your business. Most people who really want to grow a business work endlessly at first. You don't make money, because there isn't any. You don't get to become a millionaire by selling your business, because it is of no value to anyone but you. But your employees see you as just one of the guys, being in the same boat as them. Your lifestyle is very similar to theirs.

As a new manager you may mistakenly think you know what you're doing with employees. I know I did. Being an employer, like being a parent, does not come with an owner's manual. Even though one can become educated in the area of human resources, it typically takes a while to develop your style and skill set; you simply learn as time passes and as you gain experience. In the same way that some people never learn to be good parents, some people never learn to be good employers. Your employees will notice if you're a bad employer, but there's nothing they can really do about it. It's unfortunate and bad for business when that happens, and it's amazing how many people work for employers or bosses who haven't learned how to treat their people well.

If your business grows, at some point you will wake up and find you have more people than you know how to manage. Or you might realize that your receptionist, secretary, bookkeeper, or shop foreman are also acting as your personnel department. The lead workers in your shop might have been interviewing and hiring the people you need, because you're primarily looking for skilled labor, but you're not really doing good screening, training, or reviews. Your benefits program may need attention. And all these factors begin to build up, ready to erupt, and it often manifests as mumbling and grumbling from the shop floor or the office. It's easy to think that you, as the owner, have it all together and that your employees are just immature, or don't realize how much work is involved in running a business, or that they only think about themselves and never think about the business as a whole.

At the same time this is happening, you will start reaping just a few of the rewards of being an owner. You may give yourself a raise in pay, which you deserve after all the years of hard work. Perhaps business is going fairly well and you take an extra day off now and then. Employees notice. Things are good except for this gnawing feeling of uneasiness you can't seem to shake. You might buy your first new, nice car, or upgrade your house. You and your employees begin to realize that you are *not* all in this together, but nobody seems to know what to do about it, except to grumble. You naturally start to think that you just can't hire good people, or that they are unreliable. There seems to be a chasm between what you think about yourself and what you think about your employees. You remember how hard you worked to get here and you notice *the kids these days* just don't know how to work. After all, you think, it can't possibly be you; it has to be them. The problems with employees come faster than you can deal with them and the string of issues that arises seems endless. Worker's compensation claims rise, people lose more days to sick leave, or they don't return to work after a three-day weekend, and you seem to be the only one there who can change a burned-out lightbulb.

This happened to us, but there was one particular incident that caused me to take a step back and analyze what was really going on, because it really upset me. I'll tell you the story.

Early on, after our third attempt at hiring, Christmas time rolled around. My wife, Cindy, made some sandwiches and cookies and invited everyone up to our small, newly remodeled house for a long lunch. It was just a time to share together, have some food, and do something nice, even though the offerings were meager.

We had so much fun at our little company Christmas party that we decided to have a barbeque the next summer. I bought steaks, made some side dishes, and we invited everyone over on a Saturday with their families. We had a great time.

This tradition grew. One year, I bought a suckling pig and we put it on a spit and roasted it. We named the pig, Arnold Ziffle, from the show *Green Acres*. We laughed and laughed when we'd go ladle a spoon of basting juices over Arnold. I made tons of food and everyone came over and hung around all day. It was the 1980s and we had about a dozen employees. When we turned on the TV, Prince's video for "Raspberry Beret" came on; we watched it and marveled at the purple guitar we'd made. This was a highlight for us, with the camaraderie just oozing out of the backyard. We could barely contain our feelings of shared accomplishment. Boy, we were in it together in a big way, enjoying our successes as a group. We lifted a glass to the small successes we'd made as a team and repeated this tradition every summer with great anticipation.

Cindy and I bought a bigger house a few years later. We had made a good profit on the sale of our first and second homes and we were frugal with our money. Our success in home ownership, along with our good personal financial habits, made it possible for us to buy a house big enough so that Cindy's mom could move in with us after Cindy's dad passed away. Her mom also paid a small rent to us, which helped us to pay the mortgage for the larger house. This home purchase wasn't a direct outcome of the success of Taylor Guitars or of my salary, but rather it was made possible by other, outside sources of money. It was a culmination of many events in my life as well as some careful planning outside the company.

By this time, the shop barbeques, as we began to call them, had grown to where I would take three or four days off to prepare. I became an expert at making all kinds of food, but the main attraction was my homemade ice cream. I bought four ice cream churns and started days in advance. I had to buy a chest freezer to store all the ice cream. I'd make about 100 quarts and up to eight different flavors. And, by the way, if you can't make good vanilla ice cream, you can just forget making any other good flavors. It's all based on the vanilla. But I digress. The food we prepared slowly evolved into more elaborate dishes like lobster, shrimp, prime rib, mussels, clams, fish, and chicken. It was over the top and people could come as they were with their families and hang out all day. You couldn't possibly eat all the food; there was just too much. That's what a feast is; it's an overabundance, and certain occasions require a feast. This was our time as a business family to really share together and do something we normally wouldn't do.

One year, after we had moved into the new place, we worked to landscape it in time for the party. It was a new house and was surrounded by dirt the day we bought it. We installed a pool, but being a do-it-yourselfer, I contracted that pool myself and built it for a small fraction of the normal cost. You wouldn't believe how affordable it can be if you have green-cash-money to hand out to guys on a weekend who build pools all week long for their job. I built a patio after work and on weekends. I stayed up until midnight working on things. Cindy hired helpers and planted numerous plants, and we rolled out sod for an instant lawn. The sprinklers came on and everything took root. The place looked beautiful when everyone arrived. This party was geared up for over 100 people because there were 40-some employees and their families on the guest list.

People walked in and went to work on the food, jumped in the pool, and had a great time, but the comment I overheard that made the most memorable impression on me was from a group of people standing together, looking at the yard, the pool, and the patio. One of the group said, "Well, I can see where my raise went!" After everyone went home late that night and I was cleaning up, that comment kept playing over and over in my head. Among other things, it made me feel alone.

That was the last barbeque I had at my house. I realized something was different now.

This was September of 1990 and Taylor Guitars was finally starting to do okay after 16 years of hard work. We were making about eight guitars per day and even though nobody was getting rich, we had a couple nickels to spare at the end of the month.

But it felt like we were losing control of that family feeling we had created in the workplace. The new people we hired came into a small business that already had a few dozen employees and they knew they weren't in on the ground floor. We didn't make a promise or gesture that if the company does well they would share in the reward; we just put them at a bench and started showing them how to make their part of the guitar. We paid them every Friday, gave them holidays off, plus vacation and medical benefits. They looked to fellow employees in order to form their opinions of their new workplace. If the person they worked beside had a bad attitude, then the new employee could easily adopt that same attitude. They didn't know me very well and without working directly with me, they didn't have an opportunity to know me. Their work family consisted of their bench mates, and leadership from me was lacking. The people who had been there from the beginning were doing okay, but there was now an obvious difference between what they were getting out of Taylor Guitars and what Kurt and I were able to get. Gone were the days of feeling that we were all part of the same team, poised against the world, making guitars we were proud of and sharing a sense of communal greatness every time one got sold.

In some ways, it started feeling a little like *every man for himself*. I began to notice a lack of professionalism, and the workdays were filled with our co-workers trying to eek out some fun in the day. I had some serious craftsmen, to be sure, but many of the employees began to gather into small groups and made sure that they took the time to create their own fun while they were making guitars. Some of those days at Taylor Guitars reminded me of an issue of *National Lampoon* magazine, where the personal satisfaction of a workday was obtained by employees figuring out how to make the job of guitar making comical or less serious. There was a lot of goofing around.

I remember once asking people why, in all the hours they work together, did the conversation never really revolve around making guitars, or honing our craft? There was a time when we would talk about guitar making throughout the day. But those days seemed lost forever. That's about the time when Larry Breedlove left Taylor to start his own company, Breedlove Guitars. I couldn't leave, and I didn't want to leave, but this was the time when many owners would leave. Two other craftsmen went along with Larry because the old magic wasn't there anymore at Taylor. We were making progress with our product and our sales, but something not so good was happening inside with our own people. Don't get me wrong; it wasn't terrible, it just wasn't great. There was tension and some disconnect, things seemed amateurish inside our walls, and I was 15 years into it and perhaps a bit worn out.

Admitting Our Shortcomings

If we are not in this together, if there is separation between owner and employee, then what can we do to adapt to the new reality and make things good for everyone? Actually, being in it together didn't prove to be a goal that had a good reward by itself. What we needed was a way for Kurt and me to get what we needed from the business as owners, and for our employees to get what they needed from the business as employees. I have different needs from my business than my employees, but they still deserve to have their needs met. Their needs are equally important.

Also feeling the disconnect and tension within our walls, Kurt asked to meet with me. He expressed that we needed to make a five-year plan for the business. Properly done, this would be a blueprint by which we could operate and perhaps it would become a path to greater growth. He knew of a consultant who helped in these matters. I agreed that we needed a plan, and I was glad that he suggested it. We determined that if it was going to be thoroughly and skillfully crafted plan, we'd need to set aside at least a few days to do it properly.

We talked about going offsite to do the work, and checked into prices for hotel conference rooms, thinking that getting away somewhere nice would help. The price was too high, however. Instead, we settled on the empty industrial space next door to us, which contained some empty offices. We asked the owner of the building if we could borrow the space for a week. We put a card table and three chairs in an empty office with worn carpet, dilapidated blinds on the windows, and no electricity, and we got down to business.

The consultant guided us through a series of questions about our business. What was the purpose of our business? What were our goals, plans, and projects? What were our biggest problems and what would happen if we were to solve them? What changes would make the greatest difference? We tried to move past the flowery, all encompassing theoretical language and name some real goals with real words and real meanings. We ate sandwiches on the card table and hashed out ideas. We paced, squirmed, sat on the floor, and spent hours in deep discussion. We got incredibly real with ourselves and set some hard goals. Those goals became the criteria for anything we did for the next three or so years. If we embarked on a project that didn't help us achieve these new stated goals, we simply stopped doing it and refocused on working only on the goals we had established together.

One of the things we discussed during those days in that otherwise empty office space was that we didn't know how to be good employers. We didn't really know exactly what was meant by that at the time but we were willing to concede to the idea that we were just shooting from the hip and really didn't have a comprehensive plan or skill level to take care of the people working for us. It was freeing to realize and admit this, because before admitting our own shortcomings in this area, we could only blame the employees themselves. The thing is, if the whole problem was with them, there wasn't much Kurt or I could do about it. But once we decided that there was much for us to learn and implement, there seemed to be a lot we could do about it.

I began to ask myself what *I* would want if I were an employee at Taylor Guitars. It wasn't hard to imagine what I'd want. I'd want to be included, and to feel like I had a future and what that future might be. I'd want to know that I could learn new things and apply them at work, making myself more valuable. I'd want to know how the company was doing. I'd want to have some input into my job.

The big decision had been made; we were going to help take care of our employees because they deserved that in exchange for the time they devoted to furthering our company. This is where they spent their most productive years, earning a living to establish and provide for their families. If we didn't give a generous exchange, we couldn't expect their generosity in return. I wanted my employees to care for the company, and I wanted the company to care for them. Don't get me wrong; we didn't get to this point very easily. We had to vent, and complain, and suggest all manner of solutions that after thorough deliberation seemed pointless. We realized it was going to be difficult to learn how to do this, but we asked ourselves if we did learn, and were successful, would the fruits be worth the effort? The answer, after a lot of discussion, was *yes*. We felt that it was time for us to become legitimate employers, and if we did a good job in this arena, we could expand our business to any size the market would allow. We were familiar with the toll that trouble within could take on a business from our early experiences with Steve and our early employees. We had an opportunity to figure out how to create a place that was truly a good, healthy work environment. I kept focusing on the notion that if I learned how to create a great workplace with dedicated employees, we could expand our company to any size.

We worked on implementing a standard pay scale, vacation time, medical benefits, and a 401(k) program with matching contributions, bonuses, and profit sharing. We worked toward better management styles and training programs, and started better and more consistent performance reviews. We made our employees a number one priority. We adopted the mind-set that our profit would come from giving good value to our customers, not from scrimping on our employees. We worked to communicate all of this to our employees.

When we grew to about 60 employees, we hired our first human resources manager. But even before filling that position, we began to act as though we had a personnel division in place. We did our best to ensure the decisions we made and the steps we took were to the mutual benefit of the company as a whole and each individual employee.

Once, our medical insurance rates nearly doubled, without warning. It was a California-wide crisis. We simply did not have the money to afford this. Whereas many small companies paid only the employees' premium and had the employees pay for their families, we paid full coverage for both the employee and the family prior to the runaway cost of premiums. We discussed the idea of only paying the employee's portion, but weren't happy with the negative impact that would have on anyone with a family. Our solution was to pay 75 percent of any employee's premium whether they were single or had a family. This cost the single people $30 per month, and kept the increase to the employee with a family to only about $100 per month while the company's share of the increase ROSE by about 50 percent. This decision resulted in the best solution for the largest number of people and honored the needs of both the company and the employee regardless of their family status. We all paid more money, but we did it together.

You don't have to give away the profitability of the business to garner trust and respect from your employees. You just have to consider their needs, show some solid leadership skills, and be fair and generous.

Later, we were able to add company matches to 401(k) contributions as well as profit sharing and bonuses. Kurt's strong financial planning skills are what made this possible, along with our ability to make guitars profitably.

Kurt and I feel strongly that profit is for one's future, whether for a company or an individual, so our profit sharing goes directly into an employee's 401(k). If they don't have a 401(k), we open one and put the money into it. Soon, it seems, they begin contributing on their own, once they see the money that the company is contributing.

Bonuses are different; they are geared toward meeting immediate needs, so they are given to employees to do with as they please.

One of the most difficult things we had to learn, quite frankly, was how to make quicker firing decisions. We learned that part of our obligation to our good employees was weeding out the bad ones. How could we ask some people to focus and do good work while letting others get away with not doing that at all? We have all worked with people who think they are somehow Teflon coated, or fireproof, and seem to suck the spark out of everyone around them because of what they are able to get away with. I'm not referring to someone who is not as talented or experienced as another; I'm referring to a person with a negative attitude. It was our job to work toward establishing a higher caliber of people and unfortunately, that meant letting some people go.

We expected a lot from our employees, but we found a way to treat them with honor and respect and to allow them to know what to expect from us and from the job. Ultimately, it wasn't the list of what we implemented that was the key to the change. Rather, it was our change of heart that was the key to the change. Once we acknowledged that we had to learn how to be good employers, we were able to assess problem areas honestly and change the company's approach willingly if that was what was needed. If an employee was screwing up, we held them accountable for that, but we were also willing to invest in them by making the facility a comfortable place to be, and by being interested in their health, safety, and well-being.

We learned to provide leadership. I learned that the majority of employees want to be led. If there's bad news or good news, they want leadership. I learned that most employees are well equipped to handle bad news if it's presented honestly and with care. And by the same token, they don't want the good news hidden from them either.

Therefore, if we make a profit, we share it. If we don't, there is none to share. It's the management's responsibility to lead the way to profit. The employees will follow if there is a plan.

Delivering Bad News

There was a time, years later, during a recession, where we knew we were going to have to lay off some people and there was much talk among management about how much we would tell employees ahead of time. There were two camps: One felt we shouldn't say a word until we handed out the pink slips, and the other felt we should tell them as soon as possible, long before the changes were implemented. Some thought that if we told them too soon, we would wreak havoc; some might quit early, anticipating that their jobs were at risk, while some might be angry or hurt and spread ill feelings, and in general, make work difficult for us or for those around them.

My feeling was that if I were an employee, I'd want to know immediately. Heck, I am an employee, and also an owner. I knew of our impending decision and that knowledge affected my spending habits at the time. Why would I hide such important news from someone who I planned to lay off in two months time? How could I ever say that I respected my employees and their families if I was willing to withhold some of the most important news that they'd ever receive?

We told them. We told them who, why, and when. We told them how much their severance would be and what week they'd most likely be let go. We would let some people go earlier than others and we hoped everyone would stay and help until their part was finished. We helped them with their unemployment and we held a job fair to help place them in new jobs.

We explained that we wanted to treat them with respect and if we were in their position, we'd want to know. They appreciated it and overall, the transition went smoothly. Eventually, we even hired many of them back.

Our company earned a lot of respect from our employees during this phase, and this was just one example of how we used even the bad times to build our relationships with our employees.

When we host events now, employees are happy to come and share in them because they don't feel neglected at work. They are aware of the importance of their role at Taylor Guitars, and it's not a mystery to them as to how they fit in, or for that matter, how I fit in. After all this time and all the changes and growth we've been through as a company, it truly feels as though we are all in this together. I wish you could see how we work as a team when we have to produce a new model and get it to market, or fill orders that have to ship right away, or fix train wrecks in the factory, or get through a year of recession together. We work as a team for the sake of the company and the sake of our families and customers, and it feels great to everyone.

Apart from the stories of unusually negative circumstances, there are positive situations each and every day in which we learn how to better relate to our staff. We have developed a very effective training department, where people are able to learn how to do their jobs and know that they are doing good work. We continue to inform our employees about what is going on within our company, and they appreciate it.

The funny thing is that today, we have nearly 700 employees and you could ask any one of them, or any one of our visitors, or friends of employees, and you'd find out that what we have is a *family* at

Taylor Guitars, and that people love working for us. And even though I have a role as an employee of the company and work beside them, I also have a role as the owner, and nobody begrudges that in the least. We all seem to be happy for each other's successes in the company at whatever level each person has been able to achieve.

It can be done. A company can go through the difficulty of learning how to take care of its people and end up on the other side where it's good. It just takes commitment on the part of the leadership to figure it out.

We often use the saying that we are all *in this together*, and we also like to use another term for business: *family*. We say a good business has a family atmosphere. When I think about that, I think of how families can be pretty dysfunctional, and that families grow and people leave and strike out on their own, and even come back sometimes. I think that if a group of people become engaged in their work, feel like their contributions are valuable, are treated with respect, and feel safe and protected by the owners, then a real sense of family has been achieved.

Larry Breedlove sold his company to his partner and returned to Taylor Guitars, about four years after he left. We have an incredible relationship, designing and building guitars together. We're both better off for the experiences we've had as Taylor Guitars purpose-fully learned to become a good employer. Larry is in charge of a large group of people and everyone in that group is fortunate to have him as their boss. Like me, he's learned a lot and applies that wisdom every day.

We now have a huge Christmas feast and three or four barbecues a year at the factory. We hold them on-site, on the grass, and people come out for a long lunch and enjoy each other's company. I quit doing the cooking because I had bigger fish to fry. While we were reinventing our relationship with our people, I was learning how machine tools were changing in a way that would empower us to change the future of guitar manufacturing.

14 Embracing Technology

It was a dark and stormy night. A dozen Japanese journalists were gathered by the window. A typhoon was blowing in Tokyo that night in 2004. Rain was hitting the buildings sideways, and the street flowed like a river. Being from San Diego, where the rain rarely falls, I enjoyed watching nature's show. With the hurricane coming through, I was surprised at how many guests showed up for a night featuring Taylor Guitars. We had become a well-known brand in Japan by then, enough to go to Japan and attract both the press and an audience of more than 500 people for a concert featuring one of our premier players, Doyle Dykes.

We met with the press before the show, who were there with their notebooks. I'd learned a little bit about communicating with our Japanese friends over the years, who have always managed to be very direct on certain topics, including quality. We came to a point in our meeting where I knew what was coming next: "And now, we want to complain."

The first time I heard that line I was taken aback and my first response was to become defensive. But I later came to find it endearing. I realized it was odd phrasing from someone not completely familiar with the English language, and that he simply wanted to discuss quality.

During those complaining sessions, they'd ask all manner of questions, and I discovered that although they were asking questions they weren't accusing me of anything. One time, a distributor's representative asked, "We received several guitars last month and some were tuned exactly and others were out of tune! Why is this?"

My first reaction to that was to think, "Are you kidding me? I ship guitars from San Diego to Japan and you're complaining that some arrived out of tune?" But then I got a hold of my emotions and answered saying, "Well, some of them might have slipped during the shipping process." They discussed my answer with one another and then bobbed their heads in acknowledgment saying "Aso, aso." Then they wrote down the answer. They loved the details.

I came to realize that it was okay for me to assume the role of the expert to my customers. This was a new concept for me because I started out in the business so young, when all our clients and peers were older and had been selling guitars for years before I came along. They were comfortable in approaching me as if they knew much more about guitars than I did. I had grown accustomed to relating to dealers as experts, while I was just the guitar maker.

But I'd had many experiences with Japanese journalists by the time I was gathered with this group, and I had enough confidence that I could tell them what I thought. While they respected this about me, they loved to toss out the tough questions, too.

You might wonder what tough questions you could ask about guitar making in the first place. I mean, really, this is not rocket science or brain surgery. But guitar players, like many other musicians, tend to be traditionalists and care about how their instruments are made. Where we might not question what techniques a factory uses to make our tires or computers, guitar players seem to be very interested in how their guitars are made.

Guitar players like a guitar that is handmade even though it can be difficult to explain the exact meaning of the term *handmade*. There have been some pretty poor guitars made in factories over the years, so people tend to think of the good guitars as being handmade, even though there are lots of examples of good guitars made in factories. Still, people associate factories with bad guitars, and they often extend that opinion to include the idea that machines make bad guitars.

Of course, bad guitars can be made with machines or by hand. I own a factory and use machines, and I make good guitars. And these good guitars were what drew this group of journalists to our event in the middle of a typhoon in the first place.

The questions were posed that night, and I answered them all with ease, wishing to explain our processes and our guitars to give them the best understanding possible. Eventually, one journalist raised his hand and said, "We in Japan hear that you use many new, modern machines to build your guitars? Why is this? What do you say about this?" It was obvious by his tone that this question was meant to trip me up, to put me on the defensive, and to cause me to justify our use of machines.

I pondered his question for a second and responded saying, "Yes, we make our guitars using all the modern techniques and machinery that we can afford to buy. If we could afford more we would buy more machines. If there is a machine that I like for our guitar-making process, I buy it without question. Because of this decision, we have been able to continually improve our guitars and our process, and we have preserved jobs in our own country. Guitar manufacturers in Japan have not invested in their guitar factories, but rather, they have let the technology remain static, and have instead moved their manufacturing offshore where the labor is cheaper. In contrast, our production in California has grown and our quality has improved. You have very few factories here in Japan making guitars, where there once were many. I think that is a shame."

I never heard so many *Aso*s in my life. Every head was down writing my comparison feverishly.

If you know the guitar industry, you will know that Taylor Guitars holds the reputation of being the guitar maker that uses the most manufacturing technology. I was the first person to really embrace, exploit, and share the technology. But there was one who came before me.

How Francis, Adrian, Dave, and Larry Changed Guitars

The modern factory age began for Taylor Guitars one day in the fall of 1989, 15 years before that day in Japan. We'd made it through the early 1980s when disco and glam rock nearly crushed the acoustic guitar industry into so many splinters. We were emerging from the carnage as a serious player in the market. I had spent all those years since 1974 making any kind of machine or fixture that I could dream up, as well as teaching employees how to master those machines.

Tom Anderson, of Tom Anderson Guitar Works, makes solid body electric guitars in a small shop north of Los Angeles. Tom's guitars are as good as a guitar can be. We'd become acquainted and became fast friends. We loved to talk guitars. In fact, the only plane flight I've ever missed in my life was one where I was traveling with Tom. We had a connecting flight in Chicago and we were so engrossed in our conversation about guitar making that they announced and loaded our flight, announced the last boarding call, closed the door, and flew the plane away without us even noticing. Eventually, we looked up and saw we were alone and wondered how we could have missed all that.

When I say we are both interested in talking about guitar making, you now have a clear idea of what I mean.

One day, after meeting Tom at the NAMM show, he asked to come down and tour the Taylor Guitars factory. He had heard about all the nifty production methods we had developed. I was anxious to share my interests with Tom and so he arrived, and we started the tour. At some point along the way, we arrived at a machine of which I was particularly proud; it was the one that cut the slots for frets into a fretboard. I asked Tom how he did the same thing and he said that he uses a CNC (Computer Numeric Control) 3-Axis mill to do the job.

Less than a week later, I visited Tom's shop in Newberry Park, California, and I was introduced to the machine that would change my life as a guitar builder and business owner. The Fadal, named for its founders, Francis, Adrian, Dave, and Larry, was a large 3-Axis mill that could cut wood, aluminum, or steel, and was controlled by a computer. By programming it, you could saw, drill, and route nearly any shape you wanted.

I returned to the shop and told Kurt about my discovery. He arranged the financing, we ordered the machine, and within a couple months, it was ours.

Nearly every tool I'd made over the previous 15 years became obsolete once I learned to make those same parts on the Fadal. The accuracy of my guitar parts made a giant leap forward. If I wanted a brace for the back of the guitar to be shaped into a 15-foot radius curve, then I no longer had to stretch a string, with a pencil, out to 15 feet, draw the curve and then try to cut and shape up to that line. I simply drew the 15 foot curve on my screen by telling the program to make a curve of that radius. Then the computer guided the machine to cut the radius and it turned out perfect. I would fixture the work inside the machine and push a button.

In order to program it to do these things, there was software created by another company called Mastercam. It was my task to draw the various guitar parts on a computer screen in Mastercam, which, in turn, would write machine code that could drive the machine to cut the needed parts.

There was no level of simplicity or complexity that the Fadal couldn't handle, and so, one at a time, I drew the shapes of each part and began to replace my self-made tools and woodworking fixtures with Fadal operations. This created room in the shop as we removed unneeded machines, and within a couple years this single, flexible machine was doing most of the cutting of our guitar components. If all we wanted to do was drill holes in the peghead of the neck to house the tuning machines, the Fadal worked better than a drill press because it put the holes exactly where they needed to be. And if we wanted to carve the final shape of the necks, the Fadal could also do this incredibly complex task. No longer was I shaving, carving, and filing wood by hand to make each neck. Rather, I put a batch of eight necks onto the machine and it carved them all to a perfect shape, automatically, while I worked on other things.

Making guitars turned into a new adventure. It was incredible how I could sit down at my computer, draw all the parts that I wanted to make, then build some holding fixtures and watch the Fadal cut perfect parts, exactly how I'd designed them. Our productivity went up. If I wasn't there, an operator could simply load parts into the machine, push the button, and the machine would make beautiful parts on its own. The quality of our guitars immediately improved, and we were making better parts at a cost that was repeatable. Rather than have super high-skilled craftsmen making these parts by hand, the machine was doing the job. Although the machine freed up much of our workforce, there were still many jobs left that this machine couldn't address and so we deployed the skilled labor that the machine replaced into those areas of production.

Before we got the Fadal, we were making six guitars per day and it was evident that we could make more guitars if we were able to obtain the sales. One way was for us to design a guitar in a new price range that would target a market we had not been able to service before. At the time, there were no U.S.-made, high-quality guitars that sold for less than $1,000. Most good guitars were $2,000 or more, having climbed in price since the early 1980s. We theorized that since we had extra capacity, if we could add a few guitars to our production each day we could reduce costs and appeal to that market. This new machine was helping us make excellent parts at a minimum cost and we were able to make more of those parts each day for not a lot more than the price of the material. The increased production level felt good and we began to hire even more employees.

I suggested that we could build a simpler guitar, with less frills, and a simple finish, but with quality parts. This would be a model that would play and sound excellent and be a wonderful guitar for someone on a budget. We'd be competing with guitars that were imported from Asian factories for the first time. Kurt thought it was a good idea, but he was cautious; he didn't want our dealers and customers to race down-market and focus on this new price, thereby harming the sales of our existing models.

We decided that if we could attract some new customers now, with a lower price, we might have the chance to retain them as a Taylor customer for years to come. Kurt put together a program where, in order for a dealer to buy one of our new, affordable guitars, they'd have to commit to two of our existing models. It worked, and he directed a great sales program.

But even with these increased sales from offering a new lower priced model, Kurt was beginning to wonder what it would be like to build a brand rather than sell guitars one at a time. He wanted sales, yes, but he began envisioning a different kind of sale. He wanted our company to have *sails*, and he wanted to put wind in those sails.

15 Building Our Brand

M ine was a Black and Cream Heritage Softail. Kurt's was a Black Springer. They were both 1990 Harley-Davidson motorcycles. We took several trips together on them over the next couple years, getting away from the business to have a little fun and adventure.

During one trip we took through Northern California, a rain cloud followed us wherever we rode. The only time it stopped raining was when it would turn to sleet, hail, or snow. Winter arrived early in the Sierra Nevada Mountains that September. But we toughed it out because we had Harleys and we weren't about to be fair-weather riders.

One year we rode from San Diego to the Canadian border and back, over a two-week period. On my motorcycle, I could smell a guy smoking a cigar in a car a mile ahead, and we could feel the air drop from warm to cool simply because a field was being irrigated beside us. Along the Olympic Peninsula, a black bear ran across the highway in front of me while I looked down on the Pacific Ocean crashing against the rocky cliffs.

They sell good rain gear at the Harley-Davidson dealership in Seattle; gear you don't find in San Diego. I spent some money there and hoped for rain.

Being on the road together felt good; us two partners out on our Harleys. We'd worked hard for fifteen years and this trip was the first real reward we gave ourselves for all the hard work now that we were beginning to have some small successes in the business.

Kurt loved the Harley ads that he saw in magazines. One in particular was a photograph of the night sky with a line that said something about some people seeing only the Big Dipper in the sky, while others see a '59 Panhead. The Harley ad was selling the feeling you get when you ride. And the people who "got it" didn't feel like explaining it to the people who didn't. But there were plenty of people who got it.

Our Harleys were two-wheeled friend-makers. They were cross-generational and cross-cultural. I'd buy gas and a 60-year-old woman pumping gas beside me would tell me about the trip she and her husband took on a Harley when they were in their twenties. I'd drive down the road where I lived and a low rider full of Chicanos would lean out the window and whoop it up at me, "Hey Vato. . . . Cool Harley, man." They'd want to talk to me at the stoplight. A pickup full of El Cajon cowboys would roll down the window and holler, "Ride American!" and give me a thumbs-up. There was a feeling associated with this that spanned cultures and ages and Harley tapped into it and Kurt noticed.

He wanted to build a brand that elicited a similar feeling from its customers. He wanted people who played our guitars to tell stories about their guitars, to make friends with their guitars, to feel like they were part of something by owning a Taylor guitar. He wanted that brand strength to help fuel demand for our guitars so we could grow and affect more people in a positive way.

He started by searching out a local ad agency and was pleased to hear them reference the Harley ad that he loved so much as an example of advertising they thought could work for us. He wanted to take a chance and go for it, to change the way we were perceived in the market. He thought he'd start by hiring this agency and creating advertising that would distinguish us from all the other companies.

Guitar advertisements at the time were usually photos of rock stars holding guitars, or a photo of a guitar and a list of everything the company does to make theirs better than everyone else's. It was a "noisy" time in the advertising world in the sense that when you opened a guitar magazine you felt like you were being lambasted with everyone's claims. The thing was, they were all making the same claims. So how could we differentiate ourselves in that environment and not waste our effort and dollars?

With the help of the agency we hired, who really seemed to understand our mission, our first ad hit the magazines. It was a beautiful pastoral scene, with grass and a clear blue sky. In the middle of the photo stood a lone tree. It was a two-page spread ad and couldn't possibly be overlooked or confused with anything else in the magazine.

The byline read, "In its simplest form a guitar is just a hollow box made of wood. It's up to you to decide how to fill it." There was a Taylor guitar peghead with the logo peeking up into the corner of the page.

People stopped when they saw that ad. It was one of several in the "Trees" campaign. Each ad was a different photo of trees, with a different thought written. There were no guitars in these ads and no famous rock stars. One ad that I loved had a photo of a deep forest. It read, "In one pair of hands, a piece of fine wood can become a living room coffee table. In another pair of hands, that piece of wood can become the sweetest-sounding guitar. This is for everyone who has no desire to play the coffee table." This same ad's subhead read, "Some trees become pencils. Some trees become paper that becomes guitar magazines. Some trees become shoes. Some trees become Taylor guitars. Some trees have all the luck."

Another ad read, "Out of all the trees in the forest, only a few get picked to play beautiful music. Come to think of it, it kinda works the same way with people."

We were doing $3 million in annual gross sales in 1992 when we decided to hire the ad agency. Compared to where we came from, that was an honorable figure for us, but compared to the expense of the campaign that we committed to produce and run, we were investing a huge portion of our revenue into the ads. We were still awfully small to be playing such a big game.

Kurt, being financially skilled, began to work on how we'd pay for the ads and he decided that the best place to come up with the money was to earn the money.

We made a couple dozen different models of guitars at the time. Generally, more expensive models are more profitable, but also harder to sell. That doesn't mean that a less expensive guitar doesn't have a good profit margin, but it's more than just the percentage of profit in a guitar that makes the finances work. It's also the gross sales. If we could raise the income by making a higher percentage of expensive guitars, we'd have more money to work with. What if we could raise our annual sales by $250,000, for example, just by skillfully blending the right models into the mix of the same amount of guitars? That money would flow to the bottom line as profit and he could pay for the ads.

So he worked out a production mix that favored our high-end guitars; those that yielded greater profit for the company. It was skillfully planned so that we were likely to make and sell that mix. It wasn't just a list of our most expensive guitars. He cast the vision to the agency, and asked for help getting there. If he could make the right mix of guitars, and they could help in our branding so that we could sell them, we could earn the profit to cover the investment we had made in the ads, which in turn would pay dividends back to the company by helping our sales. It was symbiotic. Each task needed to work for the other to happen. It was a risk, but he took it. He felt we could make the guitars that would pay for the ads that would help build a brand and market to sell more guitars.

And it worked. Soon a second ad campaign came out that was entitled "Discovery." The campaign was based on a few poignant letters we'd received from buyers who had discovered our guitars over the years. It was their stories, skillfully compressed into a short line or two that communicated to readers what these people experienced when they began playing our guitars. They were simple stories about a person coming across and playing a Taylor for the first time and their decision to buy. Later came the "Play Ball" campaign—a concept centered around finding time to play guitar. One ad showed a guy playing ball with his son. Once the son was satisfied and the game was over, dad could go play his guitar, guilt-free.

In another, a wife bought two tickets to a game so her husband could take his buddy and she could stay home and play her guitar. There were five different ads for each campaign. It was expensive but Kurt knew deep inside that establishing a strong brand was the only way to build our future.

They were all full-spread ads, with clean designs and powerful copy. They grabbed your attention and you wanted to read them. After a period of time, our brand began to grow. People would see us at trade shows or guitar festivals and say, "I just LOVE your ads! You guys are so much cooler than the other companies." People could relate to them. It made the customer the star rather than the guitar or the artist. We didn't ask them to make their buying decision based on what famous player was holding a Taylor guitar. They could see themselves in the ads. They got a chuckle, or a laugh, or a quiet thought, and maybe a tear.

The very first ads were nominated for Kelly Awards, which is the equivalent of the Oscars for print advertising. It's an honor to be nominated and a huge achievement to win. The ad agency wins the award, not the client, but nevertheless, it was Taylor Guitars advertisements that were nominated and Kurt's vision in those ads. The first year, we made it into the top 25 finalists, which is in itself a big deal. Our ads were competing with the largest companies in the world, like Nike, Harley Davidson, Porsche, and others that dwarf our company. The campaign had succeeded in raising the bar for our whole industry. Professionals in the normal business world began to take notice of a little tiny guitar company from San Diego.

Kurt worked with the agency to produce separate ads for the trade journals—the magazines that only went to dealers, and not to consumers. This was also a bold move. Most companies simply repeat their consumer ads in the trade magazines, but Kurt and the advertising team decided that these ads should communicate to this group of people a slightly different message about the brand. Running these ads was an additional expense and took some serious budgeting, but he believed in it and figured out how to pay for it.

One ad that I loved was an ad that only the dealers would understand. Consumers would have never gotten it. The background is that Kurt was our sole salesman for years. He drove his Volvo around the country, with a trunk full of guitars, showing them to dealers. He never came home because there wouldn't have been anything to come home to. He stayed out there and called in orders as he got them. All our early dealers got to know Kurt . . . and his Volvo.

Nearly every dealer commented on our comfortable guitar necks when they played our guitars for the first time, so that became one of the design elements we became most know for. Incorporating these two elements into the campaign, the ad was a photo of Kurt and me standing side-by-side. They removed our heads from the photo and replaced them with the peg-head of our guitar necks— that portion of the guitar where the Taylor logo is and where the strings attach. There was a picture of a Volvo in the background and the ad read, "Once upon a time, two guys with great necks and a Volvo. . . . . . ." and then went on to tell our story. Only a dealer would understand that ad, and only a dealer would chuckle over it. They did chuckle, and they fondly remembered those times when Kurt came by. They liked us more because we'd produce and run an ad like that, seemingly, just for them! They felt good and they felt included. Each year for many years we would run a new campaign in the trade journals and launch them at the annual trade show. It eventually became something that nearly everyone attending the show, guitar dealer or not, looked forward to seeing. Dealers would stop by all day long just to say how they couldn't wait to see what our ad was that year, and that they weren't disappointed when they saw it.

Our brand was beginning to be known.

We designed our catalogs to reinforce the message of the ads. Kurt worked with a very talented design and branding company to make sure that the message was consistent across all our ads and that each and every step he took forward would build brand equity.

At NAMM in 1992, we moved our trade show booth and display off the noisy main show floor and into a quiet and private room. We filled the room with beautiful display cases that made it feel like an art collection, and dealers came there just to take a break. They'd play the guitars and feel good hanging around with us. They were buying in to our brand and what we stood for. It was all beginning to mean something. The ads, our conference presence, and our overall presentation communicated the quality of our guitars. They loved that we built our own guitar cases and were amazed at the furniture we custom built to show our guitars in a peaceful atmosphere in an otherwise cluttered and noisy show. They began to think we were cool and wanted to be associated with our brand.

Eventually our display at NAMM grew and evolved to the point that we had a complete stage inside our room where we held performances, with each year growing from the year before. The artists that play our guitars and whom we have a great relationship with agreed to help us by playing a show in our booth. We paid their hotel rooms and plane tickets out, and other than that they arrived free of charge just because they were on our side and because we take care of them when they're on the road or in the studio.

Just some of the artists who have performed on our stage at NAMM are, Tommy Shaw and Jack Blades, Ted Nugent, Goo Goo Dolls, Jason Mraz, Taylor Swift, Love and Theft, Serj Tankian, LeLe, Coheed and Cambria, Alterbridge, Pierce the Veil, Mana, Carina Ricco, Doyle Dykes, Shinedown, Leo Kottke, Sixwire, Christopher Cross, Everclear, and Lonestar.

About the same time that Kurt began to focus on how to build our brand, we realized we were outgrowing our factory in Santee. We needed a bigger space with greater capability, but this meant constructing another site designed to build guitars. We decided to build a new factory a few miles away in the city of El Cajon where we were able to start some serious growth. Kurt continued to build our brand as well as building the sales team to serve our dealer network.

Once we moved to El Cajon, we started a quarterly company magazine called *Wood & Steel* and wrote articles about how we built guitars, where our dealers were, and who our customers were who played them. It was on newsprint and wasn't flashy, but it was very well designed and had interesting and well-written content.

Wood & Steel magazine is a way to create community among Taylor guitar owners. The subscription is free to anyone who buys a Taylor guitar. It's written and designed by the Taylor team at our offices and includes information about our guitars, our players, and our company. Each issue includes profiles on professional and recreational Taylor guitar players; articles about dealers; lessons on how to play certain songs; tips on caring for your guitar; interesting travelogues where a guitar is involved; a Q&A with me that addresses technical guitar questions; and a calendar of upcoming Taylor events.

It connects people to the company, their dealers, the artists who play Taylor, and each other. Over the 15 years we've produced *Wood & Steel*, it has grown to a full color magazine, with incredible photography and copy, and we print about 250,000 copies of each issue. My friendly competitors in the guitar business often ask me, tongue-in-cheek, what our ad rates are because they'd love to advertise in it, saying they recognize how good it is and what deep market penetration it has.

Ten years after introducing the new concept in advertising and brand building, our ads had made it into the top 25 finalists of the Kelly awards seven or eight times. We were regulars. We had become accepted as major players in the broader business world. And we could hold our heads high because of the quality of business we were doing in the business world, not just because of the guitars we made. But even those people began to know about our guitars and buy them themselves. Professionals in business began to relate to Taylor Guitars more and more. We were respected because we had put down several roots. The bankers who financed our growth liked us because we met our budgets. The marketing community liked us because we conceived a branding plan and executed it one year at a time. The dealers liked us because we gave them good products on time, with high quality, and helped to deliver buyers to their store who had already heard of our good reputation. The music magazines liked us because we contributed to their issues and made them look better. Our employees liked us because we learned how to honor and respect them. Our vendors liked us because we paid our bills and had lasting relationships with them. The local government liked us because we followed their laws and helped clean up their air. Celebrity artists liked us because we served them well and our guitars work. Guitar players liked us because we made great guitars and gave them good service before and after the sale.

When trying to build a brand, it's not just about creating a clever ad, although that helped us along the way. Everything you do should enhance your reputation and your brand.

Some people consider branding to be how and where the company logo is written. They think their clothes, letterhead, signage, accessories, products, and advertising are their brand. That's true, but there is more to it than that. Every time a person comes in contact with something to do with your company, it should be an experience that builds the brand.

I've taught my purchasing department that we not only want to be the best supplier to our customers, but that we want to be the best customer to our suppliers. They are empowered to make that happen in many ways. Many of our suppliers do something humble, like make a special screw, or cut a limited amount of a particular wood. They don't have a brand of their own, but since we partner with them and include them into our family, they feel like they are part of the Taylor Guitars brand. I get letters every month from vendors expressing how they feel like they are Taylor Guitars; that they are part of the team just like the people within our own walls. That is a brand experience for them, and when they're out and about, they spread the Taylor Guitars message, even if all they do is mix our paint, or chrome-plate our bridges, or print our *Wood & Steel*, they are included and important for our success. When they see a Taylor on stage or on TV they say to their friends, "Hey, I'm part of that!"

Our dealers sell lots of brands, but many of them are in love with our brand, so we want to make them feel like part of our company. There are a lot of ways that we can connect besides the obvious one of delivering good guitars to them. We treat them well, we're thankful for their business, we include them in exciting news and exciting events. We do Road Shows at their store, and bring them to our factory. We "love 'em up." It's not hard to do.

We treat artists with respect. We try not to ride on their famous coattails, but rather, we try to help them with their guitar needs as job one, and then, if there is some mutual business that we can do together, great! They get the sense that we're not trying to get something from them. Consequently they end up liking our brand.

Brian Swerdfeger, our VP of Sales and Marketing, teaches our staff that everyone is a potential customer or colleague, and we want to bring a good Taylor Guitars experience to all the people we come in contact with. That means the load-in crew at the convention center when we do a show, or the truckers that take our products in and out of our buildings. It means the server at the restaurant when they see our company name on our credit card. It means the person calling with a ton of questions who is thinking that they might possibly want to buy a Baby Taylor. It means the local newspaper reporter, or the college student writing a paper on local business, or even the 4th grade class and their teachers and parents.

It was Kurt's idea to purposefully work on building a brand and he figured out what that meant. He kicked it off with how he communicated in advertising, and in other marketing materials, but he's said to us over the years that he feels the real opportunity in any business is to simply do a better job. He guided Taylor Guitars to new levels with his innovative approach to how guitars are usually marketed. He took a little guitar company and approached it as though it were worthy of branding and worthy of excellent financial planning.

I am so fortunate that I didn't have to worry about all this. Kurt did it. You might think that I was embroiled in all these decisions, but I wasn't at all. He presented finished ads, and finished plans to me. If he spent hundreds of hours, over months or years of developing these ideas, I could get the summary of all that work in 30 minutes or less. I'm not exaggerating. If he needed input from me he'd ask for it. If he didn't ask, it's because he didn't need it. That's what our partnership is like. I trust him to make these decisions.

And he trusts me, because while he was doing this work for our company I was working on other things that had to do with guitar design and the evolution of our factory, and that is a big job that needs clear vision and the same type of leadership that Kurt provided to our branding mission.

16 Innovation

W e hold events at dealers' shops around the world called Taylor Road Shows. At the shows, we display custom guitars that we bring from the factory; these are guitars that customers might not normally get the chance to see. At the events, we teach people about various models and how the different shapes of the guitar body, or the different woods, affect the tone. We show them how guitars are constructed and sometimes we bring factory technicians to service the customers' Taylor guitars if they bring them to the store for the events. Players meet each other and make friends, they buy guitars, and with the help of the dealers, we create a wonderful sense of community at their stores.

We arrived at one of our dealers in Hawaii to host one such event. We set up our service benches and got to work, meeting our customers and cleaning and changing the strings on their guitars. They were thrilled to have their guitars serviced by factory craftsmen.

As all companies that provide support to their clients inevitably discover, there are always some clients who are more demanding than others. One customer in Hawaii had been contacting us regularly complaining that his guitar was not made well, couldn't be fixed, and that we didn't know what we were doing. We tried to help him long distance, as well as through his dealer, but he didn't want to believe what we were telling him. He'd owned guitars before and when we explained to him that we could easily adjust his guitar, he insisted it was impossible based on what he knew about how other guitars are traditionally made.

Rob Magargal, one of our best technicians, was approached by this unhappy customer at the event in Hawaii. Since he was contacting us often, the customer knew we were coming, and we knew he'd be there. It felt as if a showdown was scheduled. But we didn't want a showdown; we just wanted happy customers and good guitars. A group of technicians huddled around Rob in antici-pation of this moment, anxious to see what was going to unfold. The customer took his guitar from the case, put it in Rob's arms, and while he was listing everything that was wrong with the guitar, Rob loosened the strings, reached into the sound hole, removed three simple bolts, completely took the neck of the guitar off and handed it to the customer asking, "Could you hold this for me, please?"

Shocked, the customer stopped what he was saying mid-sentence, and uttered, "What?"

Rob repeated, "Hold this, please, while I put some new spacers on your guitar."

Confused, the customer gave his consent, "Um, okay . . . ," and took hold of the neck.

Rob inserted a couple new wooden shims into the guitar that would adjust the setting of the neck, and then said, "Okay, I'll take the neck now." Three minutes after first being approached by this disgruntled customer, Rob was reattaching the neck of the guitar.

The crowd grew hushed. Rob kept working. Two minutes later, the guitar was being tuned up to pitch again and Rob handed it back to its owner and asked how he liked it now.

He liked it. He loved it. It was perfect. Game over. We turned an unhappy customer into an evangelist for our company and moved on to the next one.

This guitar was designed with our patented NT—or New Technology—neck, which was introduced on our twenty-fifth anniversary, in 1999. The NT neck was the full embodiment of the first bolt-on neck I'd designed when I was 19 years old. If this customer's guitar had been built using the traditional dovetail neck found on nearly all other guitars, the customer would have needed to leave his guitar with the technician, or possibly ship it back to the factory, and expect a long and arduous repair. The neck would have been steamed off of the guitar, chiseled to a new angle, shimmed with wood strips to make up for the lost wood from chiseling, and then re-glued to the body. It would have been expensive and time-consuming, and the customer would not have been able to walk away happy in the five minutes it took Rob to fix the guitar at a makeshift bench inside a retail store.

We didn't invent the guitar, and we didn't change its appearance or try to introduce a totally new concept to the player. We simply improved the way the neck attaches to the body. This innovation resulted in significant benefits to us as guitar builders and to our customers. It allows us to make adjustments in the factory—very minute adjustments—so that the guitars leave the factory in optimal shape. It also allows us to recapture that setting in the field, very quickly and easily, if some drift occurs in the setup.

It was hard work to complete this new design and get it into production. It required a host of highly developed, computerized operations and a robust design. Each and every operation to build the guitar, from building the body and the neck, to the finish and final assembly, had to be redesigned and consequently, retooled. All the special jigs, fixtures, and molds that we had amassed over our 25-year life span were rendered useless with this new design. It all had to be replaced. We were so confident in the new design that I gave the go-ahead to undertake this colossal project.

It took three years to build the tools we needed. During this time, we continued building guitars in our traditional manner while refitting our existing factory. Over a period of one year, we added one model after another to the new production line until all the guitars were being built to the new design. There were literally two assembly lines, or assembly techniques, in one building while the transition was being made.

When dealers received stock of the all-new NT neck design, they opened the box and saw exactly what they were used to seeing. It was radically improved in its quality and the eventual owner would be able to have the guitar adjusted or repaired very easily in the future if the need arose, but ultimately, the guitar looked the same. There was nothing sexy about it; it didn't look better—it was just made better.

When an improvement is hidden from sight, like this one, we don't experience more sales right off the bat. But as we make guitars with the new design, over time, people get an opportunity to experience its benefits—like our customer in Hawaii—and word spreads. One at a time, these stories are shared and the experiences with dealers are chalked up as positive encounters with Taylor Guitars. Over time, these positive reviews add up, and that helps us gain market share.

These types of innovations, to the guitar or even to the process, have a slow and methodical effect on the company.

Sticking Our Necks Out

Manufacturing high-quality acoustic guitars is an interesting business. Modern steel-string guitars like ours were developed in the early part of the twentieth century through innovation. Guitars were once strung with gut strings, but wanting more sound volume, makers began to use metal strings instead. This put more tension on the guitars and so the design changed until eventually, a new type of guitar evolved that could support and withstand the tension. These newer guitars were called steel-string guitars, as opposed to nylon-string guitars, or classical guitars.

But somewhere along the line, the innovation stopped. People believed that they'd mastered the design and there were no further improvements that could be made. There were some people who felt that we should no longer innovate, but rather, try to recapture what was good about the guitars of the 1930s and 1940s. These are referred to as *pre-war* guitars and are highly sought after.

But when I started building guitars, I just saw what was wrong with them. They sounded good, but they were unstable, hard to play, and very hard to service or repair. The main problem, as I saw it, was that the neck was permanently attached to the body and often, the details of that attachment were wrong. This was either because of poor setup in the factory, or because of age, which can cause the guitar to pull and change shape.

I sought to improve this part of the guitar, and so I changed the traditional way that the neck is attached. Over the years, our capabilities improved, especially with the introduction of modern computer-driven machines. If our predecessors had these same capabilities at their disposal, they would have been able to improve upon the guitar designs. But they didn't, so they did the best they could.

Enthusiastic guitar customers are interested in the guitar's construction and while they want innovation, they also typically want to see some evidence of adherence to traditional methods. Often, they speak louder regarding staying true to the old ways than they do about innovation, so it was my goal, eventually, to innovate a complete redesign of the guitar but present it to the customer in a traditional package. It worked, and with our improved quality and serviceability, the word began to spread to more and more players that Taylor is a guitar to consider.

Today, our guitars ship all over the world, so it is important to be able to service our product no matter where it ends up. As a result of this one innovation, the NT neck design, we have gained a reputation of being stable and serviceable no matter in what part of the world one might live.

Amplifying Our Efforts

Another innovation of importance is how we amplify our guitars. Customers' playing habits changed and they wanted high-quality guitars that they could easily amplify. There was a time when an acoustic guitar was amplified by standing in front of a microphone on stage. That doesn't work well, especially with modern music, which is played loud. People needed more volume and more freedom to move around the stage than a microphone provided. In the 1960s, people discovered that a *piezo* crystal element could be placed beneath the strings on the bridge and used to amplify the sound. Eventually, third-party manufacturers began making these *pickups*, as we call them, for any manufacturer, like us, to buy and install. People wanted to plug in.

We adopted this style of guitar building—designing our acoustic guitars to be fitted with electric pickups— early on, and so we gained the lion's share of this business over the years. During the development phase of this new market of amplified guitars, mostly cheaper guitars had pickups added. We were the only high-end, high-quality guitar maker putting pickups onboard as a standard feature. Old-line guitar companies were slow to add pickups to their guitars, thinking that their job was to make a nice guitar for a customer and let the customer then take the guitar to a local shop and have a pickup system put in the guitar at their own expense—and, I might add, at their own risk. By the time other guitar makers finally accepted the fact that guitar players were looking to have pickups as standard equipment on their guitars, we had already established 20 years of reputation and market share in that segment. And to make matters worse for them, the electrified acoustic guitar segment was becoming the largest, most profitable segment. We'd been addressing it from the beginning of when guitar players were asking for it. We made it easy for our customers to have nice guitars that came from the factory, ready to plug in and amplify.

In 2002, we began to feel that we should be in control of the design, production, and quality of the pickup systems that were on our guitars. We wanted to see an improved system, and we felt that we were the only people who could do that successfully for our own guitars.

We felt that by its nature, a piezo system simply would never produce a sound that would please us. We favored building a system using magnetic-based sensors because there are several existing examples of full-sounding magnetic devices, such as the phonograph needle and microphone. But there were no existing devices we could purchase and install, because nobody in the world made anything like what we were thinking. We knew we'd have to create our own.

David Hosler, one of the guitar designers at Taylor Guitars, volunteered to head up the project. He began to experiment with and invent new devices. Eventually, he developed an entirely new system that sounded better than what we could buy, but we would have to make it ourselves. By doing this, we could constantly improve the product, make our own decisions about quality, and have something that we felt brought the guitar along the path toward improved amplified sound. It was innovation at its best, and one of the more important improvements we've made to our guitars.

An interesting detail of this new design is that it would not be possible without us having first developed the NT neck. That's because a part of the system must be sandwiched between the neck and the body of the guitar and it must be accessible in the future for service. Without the ability to safely and quickly remove the neck, our new pickup design would not be able to be installed. I think it's a good lesson on how one innovation can make another innovation possible, even though the second one wasn't even on our radar at the time the first one was being developed.

In contrast to the NT neck story, when customers opened their new guitars, they saw and heard an entirely new system. This innovation helped in small ways to sell more guitars. But it also helped spawn an entirely new division in guitar players' opinions. There were supporters and detractors, whereas before, everyone was in the same boat. Now, there was something competitive and it energized the community. It's frightening, but also exhilarating, to a company when you innovate a new solution and some people love it, and some don't. Before, they neither liked nor disliked it, because there was no competition of ideas. We believe that the leader in an industry has the responsibility to innovate and we're happy to take that position. It helps us, it helps the player, and it helps the industry.

Since designing our own pickup system, we have made more electrified acoustic guitars than ever before, which probably suggests that people approve of our design. And we have recently seen our competitors take their best shot at getting some of that market share that we own. We take the competition seriously; we don't sit back and relax, even though we have magnitudes more market share in this segment than they do.

Creating New Solutions

Sometimes, innovation can be started as a result of something negative, or simply put, as a response to some bad news.

I was minding my business one day in our Santee factory in about 1988, when a letter from the State of California arrived at my desk. I opened it to find out that within a couple months, the finish coating we were successfully using on our guitars would be illegal to spray and that I had to meet a new set of compliance rules. The problem is that there was no real, quality finish for a guitar that met those standards.

My first reaction was to try to find something that barely met the standards, and that's what I did. But during that time, I also realized that a more comprehensive solution would be necessary; it was the perfect opportunity to come up with something brand new— something that had never been done before and that could help the factory as well as the environment and my new compliance issues.

I'd known that you could cure certain paints with ultraviolet lamps, and after six years of development and commitment, we were doing it. In response to the new state laws, we designed and built curing ovens, and then worked to design a paint that would work for our purposes, because again, the solution did not exist. By the time 10 years had passed, we had a very good, working system, and by the time 20 years had passed, we were applying improved coatings with robots and achieving the least amount of environmental damage that one could imagine, while making the best guitar finishes of our careers. We even won an award from our local Air Pollution Control Department (APCD). Even more notable, during the early innovation period, the director of our local APCD, Richard Smith, actually wrote new laws to apply directly to Taylor Guitars in order to give us some protection and allow us to continue our development and remain in business legally while we did so. I didn't ask or petition for this; he just did it because he believed in what we were trying to accomplish and wanted to see us succeed.

Looking back on how much failure we had with finishes at the beginning of our company, it is amazing how far we've gotten. But we got there slowly and methodically. Ten years, or 20 years will come and go, whether you do anything or not, whether you innovate or not, and whether you improve or not, so why not get going on it right now?

Innovation takes time. Innovations usually don't change people's lives overnight, nor do they add profit into the company's bottom line immediately. They do, however, put wind in the sails of a company, helping to provide a future as well as helping to differentiate your company from others. The best part of innovation often comes when you look back five or ten years on all the improvements you've made within your company walls and to your actual product, and you ask yourself where you'd be if you hadn't taken those initial steps.

I can't imagine my company today without our NT neck, Expression System Pickup, or our UV finishes. No matter how much of an uphill battle it might be, innovation can change your company's future for the better.

17 Artists and Celebrities

W hen I am at the shop, the receptionist can't find me at my desk. I'm rarely there. I'm usually off in some part of the campus working with the team, or at my workbench building something. I'm thankful for cell phones because of that. But on one particular day I was there when my phone rang. When I picked up the phone, our receptionist, Tina, said, "Bob, I have a man on the phone who is so thrilled about his daughter's playing and singing, and he really wants to talk to you."

I love calls like that, and I try to make myself available for those calls. When this guy got on the phone, I could hear the excitement in his voice. He wanted to tell me about his daughter who played a Taylor guitar. He said she was just twelve years old and that he's sure that I've heard this line before, but his daughter "really *is* special."

I remember he referred to her as an old soul, when he said that she had been writing songs since she was nine years old, and that they were unreasonably good. He took her to buy a guitar and she picked a Taylor 12-string, a big guitar for a 12-year-old girl, but that's what she wanted and he bought it for her. She played and sang her songs without ceasing and he thought she was better than average and felt she had a chance to become a real performer.

He wondered if I would listen to a few of her songs if he sent them on a CD. "Sure," I said, "I'd be happy to do that. I'll look for it in my mailbox."

It came and I gave it a spin. To be honest, I can't give every CD that comes my way full attention. There just isn't enough time. But I try to play all the CDs I'm sent. I will listen to a song for about twenty seconds and if it's not grabbing me, I skip to the next song. I listened to every one of this girl's songs all the way through, because she was good, just like her dad said. If she were my daughter I'd have felt the same way as him. This was good music.

Many people think that I'm in the music business, kind of like a record company is in the music business, but the reality is that Taylor Guitars is not a record company or a music promotion company. We are a guitar company. We sell guitars. But there are certain times in a person's music career when we can do a lot for them. When musicians are just starting out, we try to give them a push. If they make it big, we gladly stand aside and watch them soar. If their career peaks and they start playing smaller clubs again, we're here to help them as well. We like to help all along the way.

Our magazine, *Wood & Steel* goes out to over 150,000 subscribers, with an additional 100,000 that go to our dealers. So if we write an article about an up-and-coming artist, it can go a long way to getting that artist's name in front of the right people. Sometimes, we put an artist image on our web site with links to their songs, and promote their work. We can showcase them at our trade shows and put them before an audience. These venues are miniscule compared to when they reach the big time, and compared to what record labels do, but it's a real boost when they are working to become known. I like to think we've helped a few people, here and there. And I'm thankful for the reciprocal treatment we often get when a person becomes very famous and they show our guitars to their fans, with pride.

I passed the CD of this man's daughter to our Artist Relations Director, Bob Borbonus. I expressed to him that I thought the CD was really great and wanted to know how he felt about it. He loved it and immediately called them.

One of the cool things about this girl was that her name was Taylor. I'll admit, I liked that a lot.

We immediately ran an article on her in our magazine. We had her perform on our trade show stage, her mom accompanying her all the way from Nashville, Tennessee to Anaheim, California. People sat and listened to Taylor play her guitar and sing, sitting alone up there on the stage, belting it out without fear. Taylor was also beautiful, fresh, and exciting, so we photographed her and put her image our promotional material. The price list we send out to our vendors is fully designed to look beautiful. One year she was the front cover.

Scott Swift was right about his daughter. He was a dad who believed that his daughter could be a top recording artist. And, today, Taylor Swift is.

These types of relationships are the ones I love; those that start pure, combine a genuine passion for music with a passion for guitar, that grow together, and that have mutual respect. Today, Taylor is as successful as anyone has ever been. She plays our guitars in front of a colossal number of fans and our companies do business together. We support each other, and I'm so happy for her success.

This is Artist Relations; a vital part of our company. I'm not the Artist Relations Manager of Taylor Guitars.

An Extra Fret Will Do It

Zac Brown released his song, "Chicken Fried," and became a hit. I didn't know Zac but he plays a Taylor guitar; one of our nylon string guitars. Zac continued to release more hits off his debut album, *The Foundation*, and people loved them. The Zac Brown Band was playing in San Diego at the Sports Arena and I went down to meet him. He'd been working with Bob Borbonus before meeting me, but we met in his bus and became instant friends. Zac said he'd been making a living playing one or another of my guitars since he was 14 years old.

Bob had been telling me, before I met Zac, that Zac was still searching for the perfect guitar. He told me that he played our nylon string but he played in the key of Eb (E-flat), and that his guitar notes bend sharp when he squeezes the strings. It was hard to keep his guitar in tune and he's eternally frustrated. Bob felt we needed to help him.

I thought, "Okay, lots of people play in the key of Eb, but this is the first time I've heard this."

Guitars are tuned to play in the key of "E" very easily and most players don't play in Eb. Still, I'd been pondering for a month why he was having trouble with the guitar and was interested to meet him and discuss it.

We had a great time talking in the bus. We passed a small koa-wood 6-string back and forth that we'd brought down for him to see, and we talked about things we're both interested in, like camping, the outdoors, 4-wheel drive trucks and cooking. This was real conversation, and we were comfortable.

I asked him about Eb and he said, "Yeah, we tune down a half-step to save my voice. If I sing for four hours in standard tuning, it's just too high and it makes all the difference to just drop the key."

Now I understood! They loosened the strings on their guitars, like many players do, so the guitar plays in a lower key, but since Zac's guitar was a nylon string and had very little tension to begin with, the strings just turn to floppy mush by the time he loosens them to play a half-key lower. The problem was clear to me.

Meanwhile, back at the ranch, we'd just introduced a baritone guitar to our selection. A baritone plays in a lower key than a normal guitar and to accomplish this we made tooling to produce a longer neck. If you want to play lower notes you need longer strings. By making the strings longer, you can play in a lower key, just like a cello is longer than a violin, or a bass is longer than a cello.

It just so happened that the components of the neck for the baritone could easily be repurposed and mixed with the neck from the normal nylon string guitar. David Judd, one of the craftsmen working at Taylor, was able to stop what he was doing, listen to my concept, and hand build this guitar in a matter of a couple days.

Once the guitar was complete, only three days after our meeting in the bus, I called Zac and asked if he could come by the factory, since he was staying in San Diego with his family while doing his West Coast tour.

Better yet, he brought the whole family and came over to our house and our families had a great time together eating Mexican food. I have a big wok built in, with a giant burner, and it works great for fajitas. Zac went home with "wok envy" but he also went home with a new nylon string guitar that fit in his lap exactly the way he was used to, but we'd played some tricks on that guitar and the strings were longer, by one extra fret, which was just what was needed to make up for the fact that he tuned down. This guitar now had the tension of a normal guitar, even though it played in the key of Eb, and all the tuning problems were gone. Zac said that the guitar felt great, was easy to play, sounded crisp and snappy, and felt good in his hands.

Zac was back on the road with a new guitar thanks to our wonderful team at Taylor Guitars and our ability to react fast. We solved Zac's problem, and he tells people about it. I love Zac, not just because he promotes our guitar, but because he gives back. He gives back to everyone and is extremely generous to other musicians, working to help them along their career path.

I went to Iraq with the Zac Brown Band, on a USO tour. We hung out, traveled from base to base, and had a great time getting to know each other. I became friends with each member of the band and a few of us talk regularly.

Much of artist relations also involves having their guitars repaired after an accident or heavy use, getting them a loaner to use in the meantime, and being there when they need help. Artist Relations can also involve co-branding with a model that they help design, which we can both promote. Both the artist and Taylor Guitars have fun with this. Face it, wouldn't you like to see a guitar model with your name on it? Even famous celebrities are excited when they have a model designed with them in mind, because they may have dreamed about such a thing when they were young. We love it because we like being associated with successful artists.

It's from a strong working relationship that signature models have developed between us and people like Dave Matthews, Jewel, Clint Black, Jason Mraz, Ritchie Sambora, Nancy Griffith, Steven Curtis Chapman, Serj Tankian, Leo Kottke, John Denver, and Doyle Dykes, just to name a few.

Then Along Came Doyle

If I had to pick the artist who most represented the Taylor Guitars brand and who has done the most for us, I would say Doyle Dykes. Doyle has represented Taylor Guitars to more players for more years than anyone. Doyle is a player's player. It doesn't matter how accomplished you are, or how famous you are, when you hear Doyle play guitar you just say, "Wow." Doyle ministers to your soul when he plays, and people flock to hear him.

I was busy one day, too busy to want to meet another guitar player if I wanted to go home on time. But, I followed my better instincts and came up to meet Doyle. A mutual friend had driven him to Taylor Guitars from Los Angeles that day for the sole purpose of putting us together and I felt the urge to meet him.

Doyle felt the same way about his time on that day, but he acquiesced to our mutual friend and took the ride down to this guitar company he really didn't know. Doyle didn't even play acoustic guitar, he played electric guitar, but he came anyway. He played for me. I couldn't believe what I heard. He played church songs, no singing, just guitar instrumental arrangements. He heard me hum along, and so he'd play another. I hummed to that one too, since I played and sang these songs in church every Sunday.

It was a perfect storm. We had our Christian belief in common, as we soon found out. He was an incredible guitarist and I made a great guitar. If a guy plays primarily electric guitar, he will love a Taylor acoustic guitar because our guitars are so easy to play. Doyle became an acoustic guitar player that very day, in 1994, and we began to work together. Doyle was at a crossroads in his career and he chose to partner with us. We sent Doyle on the road, playing Taylor guitars to people all over the world. So many people today associate us so closely together that they might not be able to recognize Doyle without Taylor or Taylor without Doyle Dykes.

My Stint as the A&R Guy

In case you think that I'm in charge of all this, let me tell you why I'm not.

I was a young guitar maker in love with the music of John Denver and Gordon Lightfoot. I thought I would have died and gone to heaven if they played Taylor guitars. When I was 21 years old Gordon was in town for a show, so I worked it out to go backstage and show him a nice 12-string we'd made.

I got to the venue and honestly don't remember how I got back stage, but it was frightful, that much I remember. I waited and waited, and felt nervous and out of place. Eventually he came backstage from his dressing room about 20 minutes before the concert and sat down with a couple of his band mates. I was on my own, and this was my moment. I sheepishly approached and got his attention. I felt like I was invading his space and time, probably because I was. I got an instant sense that I shouldn't be there and that I was intruding.

I introduced myself and asked him if he'd like to see one of my guitars. He said okay, and I pulled it out and handed it to him. He played it for a minute and said, "Thanks, that was nice. I really need to get ready for the show now, but thanks for showing me that."

All the time this was happening, I just wished I could have hit the rewind button and gone back and made a different decision; a decision not to even come. I don't know what I thought was going to happen. Did I actually think he'd love this guitar so much that he'd toss out his old Gibson and thank me for changing his life? Maybe in my dreams, but in reality I realized what I already knew—that I was shy, and not my own best representative, and would really rather have my finger next to a whirring saw blade than to ever be in this situation again.

I took my guitar and walked out the back way. On the way out, two cute, giggly girls saw me, and with stars in their eyes said, "Hey, are you with the band?" I said, "No," and kept walking, but what I was thinking was, "No, I'm just a dork."

From then on I let other people do this kind of work because it's just not my skill. It's not my forte, although I can be a pleasant, interested, and a helpful part of the equation. As I said earlier, I'm a woodworker, and to that I've added some skills that include tooling design, employee leadership, and a general wisdom of our company and its direction, learned over years of doing this. But I'm not the Marketing Manager, nor the CFO, or the HR Director, or Director of Sales. There are vital parts of the company that are not my skill set, so I try to focus on *my* skill set and let people with the right skills command the areas where they excel. I do, however, stay involved and sometimes have the pleasure of meeting some of the great musicians of our time. In fact, we didn't really engage in active artist relations until around our 20th year of business. And during that time I'd noticed the difference between people's reactions to me and their reactions to those who worked for me. What became apparent is that when meeting someone who doesn't already know about Taylor Guitars, it was more impressive to meet an employee, a representative of the company, than to meet the owner.

Anybody can start a company, or make a CD of themselves playing and singing. That's not all that impressive. In those days if I told the banker, or even the guy at the gas station, that I was Bob Taylor and I made guitars, they'd say, "Wow, do you work out of your garage?" They never defaulted to thinking I must own a big company, or was a success. I mean, who makes guitars? Why would they think it's big or important or successful?

But if someone who worked for me handed those same people a card and said, "Hi, I do artist relations for Taylor Guitars," the person they're meeting thinks, "Wow, that must be an important job! Who's Taylor Guitars? They must be big." The main ingredient, of course, is the skill of the person doing the job. But I had two strikes against me: one, I was the owner, and two, I was shy and uncomfortable.

By the same token, if my artist relations director brings an artist to me and introduces us, it's just more impressive all the way around. One, because there is some formality, and two, because I'm obviously busy and apparently not living my life just to meet an artist. That kind of makes the artist feel comfortable, because they live their lives fighting off people who want something from them. All around, this has turned out to be a good approach and has allowed me to be in the shop more, where I do what I love and where I do the most good for the most amount of people.

The celebrity stories are the kind of "famous artist story" that everyone wants to hear about, but the real artist relation story is that we work with hundreds of artists, people you know and see in concert, and we help to keep them on the road. It's not about how many famous people I know and how many of their phone numbers I have on my cell. Rather, it's about helping performers do their art, and have a good experience with their guitar.

Since our mission is to help guitar players make music and have a great experience with their guitars, we treat everyone with respect, as though they were a celebrity. There are lots of working musicians out there, each giving it all to play good music to their audience. For every big-name superstar we work with, there are a hundred sidemen who play with those stars. And for every one of those sidemen there are a hundred players who play in a club or in church every Sunday. We serve more worship leaders who play guitar in church every week than probably any other segment of pro players. And there is more live music heard in church each week than anywhere else.

And then there is the hobbyist, like me. The person who plays for themselves, along with their friends, for their own enjoyment. I get letters from these people every day. They are 90 percent of our customers and in the end, the most important. As the singer-songwriter Michelle Shocked once said, "Music and politics are both way too important to be left to the professionals."

Working with artists is a microcosm of working with dealers or consumers. We have customers who are just regular people who buy guitars from us like you wouldn't believe. I've had customers buy custom guitars, one right after another, and one day you look and realize that person has spent $100,000 in one year buying our guitars. How did we treat that person the first time we met them. Did we treat them with respect? Did we take them seriously? At Taylor Guitars, we want to treat everyone well, whether it's their first guitar they've purchased, or their twentieth.

I've had hundreds of customers tell me that their guitar got them through the worst parts of their lives, and that playing music brought them back from the brink of cancer, or divorce, or the death of a child.

You Have to Meet This Guy

Sometimes a very important person, a celebrity in your world, walks through the doors of your business and it's obvious as to who they are. But most people walk into your life and you don't know them at all, and they deserve to be treated well. You should treat your customers as though they are important, because they are. You never really know which dad of a 12-year-old girl is asking you to listen to the first songs of a future Taylor Swift, or which customer will use their guitar to minister to a cancer patient, or when your very own Doyle Dykes will walk into your life.

Zac Brown just recently told me a story from many years ago, when he sent his guitar back to us after several years of hard, hard use. He made his living with that guitar in local clubs, bars, and honky-tonks. He said when he got his guitar back from us, we'd replaced his worn case, and had refurbished the guitar beyond his dreams and expectations. There was little or no charge for the work, and he was "nobody" back then. He never forgot that moment.

Like I say, you want to treat everybody like a celebrity.

18

In 10 Years, We'll Be Glad We Did

"You started a shop in Mexico? What's that all about? Why would you do that? What's your plan?"

These were the questions flying at me, over and over. We'd made a decision to start a small shop in Tecate, Mexico, right across the border from San Diego.

Our factory is located in the east part of San Diego County, a city called El Cajon. Meaning "The Box" in Spanish, El Cajon is in a flat valley surrounded by hills and mountains on all four sides. We moved our production to El Cajon in 1992 when we outgrew our factory in Santee, which is located right next to El Cajon in that same valley. About 20 miles south of us is the Mexican border of Baja California, Mexico. The Mexican city of Tijuana is right on the border of San Diego, along the Pacific Ocean and the town of Tecate is about 45 miles east, along the border and about a 35-minute drive from our factory in El Cajon. My house is exactly half way between Tecate and El Cajon.

A couple dozen of my employees live in Mexico and drive to the United States each day to work at Taylor Guitars. I love Mexico. I love the people; they have taught me, through example, to be more polite when I talk to strangers. In Mexico you can't simply walk up to someone in a store or a restaurant, or wherever and say "I'll have," or "I want," or "Give me this or that." You say hello first and exchange some pleasantries. It's nice. I do that now, and I learned it from those employees.

As I mentioned earlier in the book, we began making our own guitar cases, and that the reason why our suppliers stopped making cases was because of the high labor cost and the low sales price and volume. The labor costs associated with building our own cases had been creeping up after eight years of production, and so we began to consider the prospect of making them in a factory of our own a few miles away in Tecate.

In early 2000 we built a small factory in Tecate, moved our equipment, and staffed it with a fledgling crew, reassigned those who had been building cases in El Cajon, and toughed out the first couple years. It was difficult starting with nothing and trying to build something down there, but that was how we did everything. We had to hire new people, in a different country regulated by different laws and having a different culture. Even the simplest things like shipping, or waste disposal, or hooking up electricity and phones were difficult; there was so much to learn.

During the first few years people asked me over and over what my plan was. A couple times I tried to explain and then I came up with an answer that satisfied almost everyone. My answer was, "In ten years, we'll be glad we did."

I didn't have a master plan to share with them. I had a plan for what it would take to get started, and being able to continue building our cases was enough of a reason to try. But ten years have passed and now we are glad we did. We have a robust factory there that is an exact copy of our El Cajon factory. We have over 250 employees and we still make cases there, but we also make nearly 400 guitars there every day, as well. Those guitars were designed for Tecate production so that they could hit a specific price range. The guitar models produced there are not what we would be able to make in the United States because the price we charge for them is too low to support American labor rates.

Many of the Mexican employees who once had to drive from their homes in Mexico to our El Cajon plant for a decade before were reassigned to Tecate. Now they live and work in their hometown, as supervisors, trainers, and foremen for the Mexico plant, while still earning U.S. wages. Because of the development of our Tecate plant, we are able to make guitar models that an entirely new market segment could afford to buy and enjoy. Before, only people willing to spend a lot of money on a guitar could buy a Taylor.

Interestingly enough, the sales volume of the higher-end guitars is at an all-time high now, even though we offer less expensive guitars from our Tecate factory. Together, both levels of guitar work to build our brand and our customer base.

While we didn't embark on most of our adventures thinking, "In ten years we'll be glad we did," there are so many developments and successes we've experienced where we could look back and identify a decision we made to commit time and energy and resources that paid off in ways we would have never imagined.

I told you the story of embracing technology with the purchase of our first Fadal CNC machine. That decision from so long ago led to us buying and learning to use lasers for more intricate parts of our guitars, and robots to do laborious, yet highly skilled tasks like spraying and polishing the painted-on finishes. All these years later, we operate nearly fifty Fadal machines and are one of their largest customers.

When Kurt and I decided to learn to become better employers, better bosses, better leaders to our staff of forty people, at a time when we were mostly frustrated with them, we only hoped that it would be worth the effort. Ten years, and more, have come and gone and I can report now that we have nearly 700 employees who are dedicated to and concerned about the company. They put forth their best efforts each day, and when I walk through the shop they are happy to see me. They tell me about their kids, or the classes they're taking to learn something new, or the new position they were advanced to. They show me their latest work on guitars and ask how I'm doing. It's very satisfying and I'm glad Kurt and I made those changes all those years ago. We were at a crossroad then, and we took the right road.

When we took a deep breath and redesigned our necks, having to retool the entire factory to make this single change, we felt it was good for our future. It cost us three years of singular focus in the factory and a few million dollars. Guitar shops don't typically have a few million dollars lying around, but we made sure we were profitable so that we had money to invest into that project. We never would have imagined that because of that design change, we could innovate a whole new way to amplify our guitars with our Expression System pickups. And we never would have guessed that those pickups would pave the way to a new model of guitar—the T-5, which was a whole new category of guitar that could play both acoustic and electric sounds. This guitar won player awards, and sold in record numbers.

Many of you reading this might have seen a GE Capital TV ad featuring me and our GE rep, Deb Barker, walking through the Taylor Guitars factory. Our most recent print ad had just won the Gold Kelly Award and the ad agency for GE was at the award show. They were in discussions with GE Capital about a certain type of commercial they'd like to run that included some interesting customers of theirs. They noticed our ads, and that we'd won, and decided we were exactly what they needed. Meanwhile, people at GE were thinking of us for the spot, because of their great working relationship with us. Kurt made a bold move with the "Trees" ads we had run 18 years earlier and that hard work paid off in ways we'd never have imagined. Most importantly, as I've written, we built our brand with Kurt's direction, but as a result, Taylor Guitars was featured in a television advertisement that probably cost what we would spend in 20 years of advertising ourselves.

Ironically, I'm writing the pages of this book while in Amsterdam, as we start our own European Division to serve all of Europe with sales, customer service, repair, and warehousing. It's a new step for us, and once again we're in a foreign country figuring out the laws, the culture, and the logistics. But I now have ample confidence from our successes of the past, that in ten years we'll be glad we made this move.

Ten years ago I started a project to learn how to make nylon-string classical guitars. These are different guitars than the steel-string guitars we are famous for making. We put together our team and worked on prototypes but we never made a guitar that was impressive. Simply put, we didn't know how to build good classical guitars and the secrets eluded us. We stopped the development.

Recently we started the learning process again. This time I sought the advice of a friend of mine, Pepé Romero Jr., who is a talented young classical guitar builder here in San Diego. He was willing to help me years ago, but I put it off, in effect, wasting much of the last ten years. But we started, and he showed me what was missing in my knowledge about building this style of guitar and together we made some very successful prototypes.

Armed with the knowledge that I gained from Pepé we are now developing our own ideas about the classical guitar. Just like we developed our own style of steel string guitars and found an audience for our those guitars, one day we will serve people who like to play the classical style of guitar. It might take ten years but I like to say that time goes by whether you do something or not, so why not start?

We are doing the same with solid body electric guitars. We introduced them into the market four years ago. The guitars are good and they sell well. We continue to innovate and introduce new models. We are not shattering any sales records for our industry, and we don't expect to, but we are four years down a path that we know will grow to something powerful.

I've also learned what can happen when you don't start, take a chance, and see things through to the end. Cindy and I lived in the third home of our marriage for twenty years. Cindy loves avocados and wanted me to plant her a tree in the back yard. I argued to her that it takes too long for it to produce fruit and I procrastinated it so long until we finally moved. We could have had ten or fifteen years of avocados if I'd gotten started with that tree in the first year. I could have planted it five or ten years after she asked, and still had avocados before we left that house.

Taking that chance, getting started and seeing new plans and projects through is the only way you will get to the point where you can look back and say you're glad you did. I blew it on the avocado tree. I passed up my opportunity to start. But with Taylor Guitars I jumped in and started the projects that would change our future and I'm glad I did.

19 The Third Owner

There is a deli up the street from the Taylor Guitars factory in El Cajon, California. It's the only place to get food within our industrial park of concrete tilt-up buildings and green landscaping, all watered, I might add, from a substantial water district that didn't exist one hundred and fifty years ago. Of course you can drive two miles from the factory and arrive at lots of eateries, so don't feel bad for us, but this is the only one in the park. Today you wait in line to get a sandwich. It's crazy-busy, like a deli in Manhattan. The fire department drives their trucks there in order to buy sandwiches. The fire department isn't even close to this deli. Policemen eat there and congressmen too, right next to guitar makers and people from the other businesses in the park. Heck, just the people that come for the Taylor Guitars factory tours make the line long enough for me to have to wait when I go. It's called "Hilltop Deli" and Anne owns it.

Anne is the third owner.

The second owners, Nikki and her husband, jumped in with both feet, investing lots of their money and time because Nikki always dreamed of a deli. It was called "Nikki's Deli" back then. They had fewer customers than Anne does. If they had more customers, they could have made it. It didn't appear they were doing anything wrong, but a deli in those parts needs time for people to figure out that it's there and that they want to drive their fire truck over for a sandwich. To me, the tuna tasted the same with all owners.

Nikki and her husband were so excited when they bought the deli from the first owner. I can't remember his name, but he was enthused as well. Back then, when I'd stop in to grab a sandwich I never had to wait. In fact, they jumped off their stools where they were waiting to prepare my order. He often had his kids there as well helping; little businessmen they were, each and every one. They gave me business cards and said, "Thank you Sir!" Their dad, the proprietor, found out I owned Taylor Guitars and wanted to give me sandwiches for free, but I couldn't do that. I didn't need a free sandwich. I wished they were around back when we were trying to make a go of it in Lemon Grove; I could have used a free sandwich back then. But celebrity is another chapter.

The deli was starting to get established when Anne bought it from Nikki. I'm not saying that Anne isn't a better businessperson than Nikki or the man who started the deli, but the equity that the two previous owners built before her was a springboard for her and her deli. By equity I mean something you own or create that is helping you get where you want to go. However humble it was, the equity established by the two prior owners gave a good start to the business—one that cannot be measured, but surely exists.

Our Hills and Valleys

I've always noticed the change in ownership of our local business; what a new owner does differently, why the old owner left. In the same way, but in a broader sense, I'm intrigued by stories of the history of the El Cajon and it's neighboring town, Spring Valley. I live in El Cajon, but right on the border of Spring Valley. My partner Kurt once gave me a very cool book about the history of Spring Valley called *Our Hills and Valleys*. One thing that made this book special is that one of the early settlers was a photographer from Chicago, so the book was full of very old rare photographs. They were incredible; they were images of places I know today but taken many years ago. It's amazing to me to know that people lived here that long ago, saw the same sunset, felt the same heat, and lived out their hopes and dreams in this place just like me.

The book reveals the colorful past and the ambition of the settlers who came to the valley to create a life for themselves. Our water district sits atop a spring nearby and delivers water to the area. When the first settlers arrived, there was a man who filled bottles there, sold it as elixir water, and became wealthy, only to die penniless. The nearby neighborhood called Dictionary Hill got its name because many years ago, a developer distributed the land by giving a parcel of land to any individual who bought a set of encyclopedias. It was originally called Encyclopedia Heights and one day they up and changed it. The mountain called San Miguel, which is across from my home, was the location of one of the largest land swindles in San Diego history.

It was more than twenty years ago that I read this book, but even then what jumped off the page for me was that it typically took three owners of each ranch, or homestead, before it took hold and before a family was able to stay and make a living.

Around the 1870s, families from across the country began leaving the security of Chicago or Philadelphia or wherever they were living, and made their way across the country in a wagon to arrive here in Spring Valley, some twenty miles east of San Diego. They'd homestead a plot of acreage and start to work the land. Water wasn't easily found in many places even though the little valley where I live sits atop the second largest aquifer in San Diego County. The landscape was scrubby and dry, and even the river bottoms were sandy most of the year. They came and settled with limited resources, having only so much money and so much time, and when that was used up they hoped to be well on their way to sustaining themselves with their land.

But it didn't seem to work out for most of them in this area. The laws of nature were against them, and after four or five years they'd give up and sell their property to the next family with the same dream, and they'd move west to the city of San Diego and get a job and an apartment. The weather there was cooler and moister, and there were jobs so that people could make livings.

The second family would move onto that piece of property, but when they arrived with their limited resources they didn't have to build a dwelling because it was already there. Maybe they'd improve it, but they could do that when they had the time and money; it didn't need to be done immediately. And the peach, loquat, avocado, and orange trees were now five years old and starting to produce when they got watered. The flume to water the farm was partially constructed or maybe just needed repair. They poured their sweat, time, and money into the ranch and seven years later moved to San Diego, selling their dream home to the third owner.

The third owner made it because they had a head start. They even had neighbors who were third owners and more able to help them because they weren't so destitute. Their advantages were tremendous. From reading the stories, it appeared that the third owners worked as hard as the first and second owners; it's just that they had enough of a head start to succeed.

There were certainly some first owners who made it all the way. They came with more resources, or just by luck were given more resources. Some struck water easily. Some had good health. Some didn't have the coyotes kill their milk cow and chickens.

When I first read the book about the settlers trying to establish farms in Spring Valley, my business wasn't a huge success, but I keyed in on this idea: however meager something is at the beginning, it has value and probably worth far greater than one might ever realize. You would not be able to put a high price on a new business. In fact it's a low price, evidenced by how little money people receive when they sell their failing businesses.

After reading that book, I decided that I wanted to be the third owner of my own business. I wasn't going to give up. I didn't want someone else to succeed on what I'd started and worked so hard to get off the ground, even if I'd only gotten it an inch off the ground. And when we were facing difficult times, I would think back to that book to fuel more commitment and motivation within myself.

There was a time, around 1980, when we were still struggling to make the business viable, that I accepted an invitation to sell Amway. I was lured by the promise of the money and freedom it could give, if I committed time and energy to it. I read testimonials about how a person could do it part time and make a decent amount of money, or if you really wanted to go all the way, you could dedicate your life to it and become extremely wealthy. After giving the first presentation I felt like this probably wasn't my calling. I asked myself, and my wife, if I was willing to put time and energy toward this other goal, why not put that same time and effort toward my current business? If I could come up with an extra fifteen hours a week to sell Amway products, why not just put that time into Taylor Guitars instead? Why not double down on my own bet. And that's what I did. Some other person could get rich on Amway, but it wasn't going to be me because I was a guitar maker and believed in myself more than I believed in Amway.

During those years, each time I got interested in something else that would require some commitment from me to reach a reward, I used that energy to renew my commitment to Taylor Guitars.

I've also used this vetting process to evaluate if a new idea we had was worth pursuing. We'd have an idea and get excited about it but before we implemented it, I'd say, "Just before we start on this long journey, I'd like to ask ourselves two things: One, are we going to finish this, and two, if we believe so much in this new idea, is there something else similar to it that just needs more commitment that we've already started?" In many ways I was asking myself if it would be beneficial to become the second owner, or the third owner of one of our own ideas that we were going to let die.

An exercise like this can be tricky because, as I wrote earlier in the book, we must also learn to let go of the things that aren't working. But used properly it can become a filter to examine ideas and to focus energy so that you gain equity rather than have lots of things started with none of them paying off.

What you need to commit to might be that employee-training program that you've started twice with good intentions but have not implemented yet. Perhaps it needs one more, good old college try to get it over the hump so you can start seeing the benefits. It might be that quarterly company magazine that you started two years ago and have only done two issues. If you still believe that it will be of great benefit, revisit it and see how close you are to completing it so that it becomes another piston of your business's motor firing, helping it to get where it needs to go.

There were so many successful initiatives within our business, that had to be started two, three, or four times before we were able to get them to take hold. But with each start we made a little more progress. It has not been my experience in life that we can implement a new idea and get it right and successful the very first time every time. How many times has your company put off the "go live" date of your new web site or ERP system? Ours has put it off many times.

I tried hiring employees three separate times, getting rid of everyone between those attempts before I was in a position to successfully employ them. I could have decided during one of those that employees are bad and you can't run a business with them. But I believed in the idea that employees would be good, so I kept attempting it until I got it right.

It took three attempts to get my training program up and functioning. The first couple times we just quit doing it because it was easier to cope with that day's work without having to spend the time building a way out of that day's problems, even though we knew that training was the key.

I had to implement a new production model a few times. I believed in a lean, just-in-time production model, but I'd try it out, it would fall apart, and I'd try again. Eventually, with each attempt I'd get it more right and less wrong, until finally it became understandable to my staff, and we enjoyed the benefits in the way that we'd hoped.

Being Your Own Third Owner

You don't have to own your own business to apply this thinking. You could be the third owner of your own job. I've seen employees who've gotten used to getting paid for their time, rather than their results, and they come to a point where they're not about to give of themselves toward a goal without making good money for doing it. I've witnessed employees who refuse to put forth effort to prepare for opportunity where they work, yet be willing to start over at a new job that requires a new education or perhaps pay cut, or unpaid working hours, because that's what would be required to qualify. I wonder why they're not willing to invest in themselves and come in to their current job saying, "Hey, I went to night school and earned this degree in production management," or "I taught myself to speak Spanish," or "I finished that training program on weekends and I think we could implement it now."

People read my story about working for years at total risk without pay and admire me for that. Yet, the thought would never cross their mind to work a year's worth of Saturdays without getting paid to enhance their worth at their current job. They think it's too risky. Really?

I've counseled friends who complain about their current job, and talk about starting over. But, if they are willing to put more time and energy and take on the risk involved in doing something else with someone else, why not put that work into where they are?

I had an employee, and I'll call him Bill, because his name was Bill. Bill wanted to be used more, and would come to me saying that he didn't think he was being used enough. He wanted to be involved in more exciting things and thought he could offer so much. Problem was, Bill had a hard time getting the job done that he was assigned each day, and he was qualified for that job. He spent time thinking about doing other things that he wanted to do. He finally had enough and came to my office. I'm okay with that, and everyone at Taylor Guitars is free to do that.

Bill made his plea and I assured him that the exciting stuff he was talking about was, itself, a lot of boring things added together before it got exciting. He still wanted an assignment, one that would get him closer to what he felt was the inside circle. I gave him an assignment because just the day before, we'd put a guitar in his department that was a study-case. It was a guitar affixed to a fixture plate with measuring devices touching it everywhere. It looked like some hospital EKG, or that pinhead character from the movie *Hell Raiser*. The project involved watching the dials over time and noting what moved on the guitar while it settled in to its own string tension. It was important. I put Bill in charge of it, and I asked him to make the recordings, keep a chart, and report them directly to me. That in itself would make him understand guitars better and might be the path to broader contributions to our team. The task would also draw him closer to the inside team, having a little more to offer other than labor.

Six months later Bill had taken two recordings and one of those came after I prompted him.

I have another employee named Ed Granero. Ed sees what needs to be done at Taylor Guitars. About the time I was ready to meet with Bill and ask why he was not being more proactive about our experiment, Ed walked by me in the hallway. He said, "Hey Bob, I was thinking. I noticed you put that guitar up there on the shelf with the dial indicators all over it. I figured that some measurements would be good so I made an Excel file and recorded its movements every week for the last several months. I'll e-mail it to you if you're interested. If not, I'll keep it in case you gain interest later on. See ya. Have a good day!"

Well, what can I say?

Maybe Bill felt putting forth that effort without a clear agreement as to the reward for it was not an attractive proposition. Maybe he felt he'd be working for nothing, and would just be wasting his time in the end. Maybe it's time for another Ed story.

Ed kept taking the initiative to do things on his own, besides his job, which he always completed. Pretty soon Ed got *asked* to do things besides his job. Soon those projects became big, to a point where he was the project manager for the construction of our new buildings as we added them to our campus, as well as the development of new products; all, multimillion-dollar projects.

We had a meeting once to discuss the outfitting of our visitor's center. We were all there and Ed was a couple minutes late. Someone asked if we should start, and I replied, "No, I don't want to start without Ed. In fact, I don't want to do much at all without Ed." We laughed, because everyone knows Ed. Ed arrived right as the chuckles were dying down and someone said, "Ed, you should ask Bob for a raise. He was just talking about how much he loves you and doesn't want to work without you!"

Ed tossed his folder on the table and sat down saying, "I *don't* ask Bob for a raise. That's why he loves me!" Then he started the meeting.

Ed has been the third owner of a lot of projects at Taylor Guitars. He gets raises, which I'm happy to give. He makes a good living. He's primarily a woodworker, and he's smart. He's taken on colossal projects that others at Taylor have given up on and led the way to completion, but his main love is guitars and always comes back to that when other departments are done borrowing him.

The number three isn't the important part of this lesson. But it does make one wonder why they say, "The third time's a charm." Whether it's a couple attempts or several, if you believe in your idea, and there is something solid about it, you can come back and start it again. But you must identify the ideas not worth giving up on, be prepared to try again, and not be discouraged if something doesn't take off right out of the gate.

There seems to be a lot of formulas for success out there, and most of them are true and have much merit. But what is common to just about all of them is the positive effect that hard work, dedication, and experience has on your success. Perseverance, believing in what you do, and having the passion is what will see you through the tough times. Success takes time to grow, but grow is what it does.

Whether you are the owner or an employee, take chances, believe in your ideas, and don't give up. You can be the one that sees your plan succeed. And there is opportunity in finishing what is started, and getting something to a point where it produces, whether it's the water well and fruit trees in nineteenth-century Spring Valley, or a sandwich shop, or a project at your company.

As Sophie Tucker said, *"I've been rich and I've been poor, and believe me, honey, rich is better."* It makes me laugh whenever I hear that quote. The struggle to achieve success is not something anyone wants to go through, but for most people to become successful, or to learn to be an expert, there is always struggle involved. That's the part of your story when you work for nothing, when you put out more than you take in, and when you wonder why you're doing it in the first place. But you still do it because you love what you do and you believe in it.

Everyone has ideas, but few ever cultivate those ideas into a passion, and even fewer pursue their passions. If you are one of those few, you know, too that the path to achieving your goals can be fraught with pitfalls. It is often a lonely path since you are the one with everything on the line and the only one up late at night or during holidays trying to make it work. It takes hard work, dedication, and some problem solving along the way, but you can achieve your goals if you stick with it and make adjustments to your course as you go. It can feel like you take three steps forward and two steps back, but as you close in on your goals, others will join in to help you because they'll recognize that you are providing opportunities that can help them too. You'll realize you have become a leader as a by-product of achieving your goals.

You'll make mistakes along the way, as you learn. You'll have setbacks and embarrassing moments. Sometimes a would-be top chef has to make big scary flames in the kitchen while their hungry mind and imagination is being fed. Those flames almost always get put out. Sometimes a kid who wants to build cars blows the engine, or wastes hundreds of dollars in material by mistake. They recover and move on. You can't just wait for some safer time to learn what you need to know, you have to learn now with whatever means are at hand. I am so thankful for being allowed to do that at that young stage of my life.

There were many people along the way who helped me. I can say that by implementing Agostino Loprinzi's concept of building one guitar at a time, we learned to run a guitar factory with the most accurate shipping schedule in the industry, and our dealers would back me up on that one. I don't think I could even count the hours that Greg Deering and I spent designing tools and methods of construction; he for his banjos, and me for my guitars. Having a buddy to keep you going during the late nights is priceless. Along the way, so many players and artists told people about their Taylor guitars and helped spread the news, almost as though they had stock in our company.

The good things that have happened to me have exceeded my wildest dreams. When I was in junior high school, listening to my favorite band, Creedance Clearwater Revival, I would never have imagined that John Fogerty would recognize me as a friend, as he does now, when I see him at a concert. When I bought my first piece of mahogany I wouldn't have thought that my mahogany purchases would eventually grow to sustain a few village communities in Honduras, or that my rosewood purchases would support 28 families in East India, like they do now. When I made that first guitar, I would not have thought that I would co-found a guitar company by the time I was 19, and together with my partner we would build one of the most successful guitar businesses in the world.

When we first started out, we were only building a few guitars per month. As I write this, thirty-some years later we have surpassed five hundred guitars per day. Our factory uses well-trained craftspeople using sophisticated computer driven machines to make our guitars. That's one reason I make tools; to allow the average skilled person to be able to make guitars. And because of this decision we were able to slowly expand our business over the years and include other people. The quality that we currently produce in our modern factory is so much better than I could do by hand back then. I was a good guitar maker even back in those days, which was a rare skill to have, but we're currently making nearly perfect guitars, with normal people in the shop, and in a profitable amount of time. We have come a long way, but I am still in the shop everyday doing what I love—building guitars.

I can tell you this; you're not going to be an expert at making things, especially growing a number one factory of high quality guitars if you're not interested in how other things are made and how they work. Starting early is best, and it's these innocent interests, often as a youngster, that pave the path to more focused interests as an adult, and so it's good when we allow our kids to dive in when they feel like it. That is what my parents did. That's how my school system operated in those days, making shop classes that gave me hands-on experiences, and challenged my brain, a mandatory part o my education, and I'm very thankful for that.

Now I have become known, worldwide, as the person who re-invented guitar necks; which I have, and it ended up being much more than the shape of the necks, but rather the entire method of attaching them to the body. Today, you'd have to find a very grumpy, Taylor Guitar hater, to hear anyone deny this. Nearly everyone now, who plays guitar and knows the top brands, whether they prefer our guitars or not, will tell you that Taylor not only improved its own necks but caused the entire industry to take a look at their guitars and make changes for the better. I would not have thought that would be an accomplishment of mine, when I was making my first guitar in Mr. Kaiser's woodshop at Madison High School in San Diego.

Some people leave their job at the end of the day, totally beat, after eight hours. I've seen those same people start their own business and work fifteen hour days on the energy of owning something them-selves. I am pretty sure that much of my early story was fueled by energy that came from working for myself, along with my unfettered passion for making guitars, tools, and machines. It also didn't hurt that our customers, those that we did find every once in a while, loved their guitars. Letters of praise would arrive in the mail and I have to tell you that alone can keep a guy going emotionally.

But what if you're calling is not to be a business owner? These ideas still apply. I can tell you this; business owners are looking for people who take ownership and help the business move ahead. You can make yourself indispensible by learning what the company needs and providing that.

My daughter, Minét, told me that she never would have thought she'd enjoy reading a business book, until she started her own clothing boutique with her sister Natalie. Then Minét read a business book about the famous designer, Coco Chanel, and told me she couldn't put it down. She realized that she could read a business book when it mattered and when it was on topic for her.

Minét and Natalie are starting their own business life, and if this book helped only them it would be worth my effort, but I write it for everyone who finds themselves in the same boat as Kurt and I were in during those tough times, or at the crossroads we came upon, like the day we decided to learn to become good employers. That was one of many times when we decided to get in for more, rather than to get out for less. I write it in the hope that our stories will help.

Much of what I've learned in business has come through observation and experience. I usually don't learn much unless there is some kind of application to the lesson. Like many people, I learn on an as-need basis. Information can go in one ear and out the other unless it's something I need to know. What is boring information one year might become fascinating the next only because it applies to what I'm trying to accomplish. Often that information is initially revealed to me in the form of a story of someone else's experience before I delve into the textbook version of what I want to learn. It is why I've come to tell stories about business rather than cite formulas for business success. I wouldn't begin to know who is going to read this book or what they will learn at the time they're reading it, but I believe that someone might learn something useful from my story, or concept that I propose, and as a result begin their own journey to success as I did when Augostino Loprinzi asked me if I really wanted to make half done guitars. It was just what I needed that day.